Copyright © 2010 National Fire Protection Association®. All Rights Reserved.

NFPA® 30B

Code for the

Manufacture and Storage of Aerosol Products

2011 Edition

This edition of NFPA 30B, *Code for the Manufacture and Storage of Aerosol Products*, was prepared by the Technical Committee on Aerosol Products. It was issued by the Standards Council on June 1, 2010, with an effective date of June 21, 2010, and supersedes all previous editions.

This edition of NFPA 30B was approved as an American National Standard on June 21, 2010.

Origin and Development of NFPA 30B

Prior to the development of NFPA 30B, *Code for the Manufacture and Storage of Aerosol Products*, fire protection requirements for the storage of flammable aerosols were set forth in NFPA 30, *Flammable and Combustible Liquids Code*, where they were treated as Class IA flammable liquids. During the late 1970s and early to mid-1980s, because of both actual fire incidents and full-scale fire testing, it became apparent that flammable aerosol products presented a severe fire challenge. Industry initiatives led to further full-scale fire testing and, eventually, to the establishment of an NFPA Technical Committee Project specifically directed at providing fire protection guidance for both manufacturing facilities and storage facilities.

The Technical Committee on Aerosol Products began its work in January 1988. The committee formed two task groups, one on manufacturing and another on storage, to draft the technical language of this document. The results of the efforts of the two task groups culminated with adoption of the first edition of NFPA 30B at the 1990 NFPA Annual Meeting.

The Technical Committee on Aerosol Products continued to work on improvements to NFPA 30B. The second edition was published in 1994 with several major revisions to clarify the document's requirements and to more accurately reflect the fire behavior of aerosol products, particularly with regard to the classification of aerosol products. The Technical Committee on Aerosol Products then continued its work, resulting in the 1998 edition — the third edition of NFPA 30B.

NFPA 30B implemented extensive revisions for the 2002 edition. A major testing effort resulted in a complete revision of the wet-pipe sprinkler tables and their associated reference figures. The Technical Committee added 12 new tables to Chapter 6 (deleting the 5 tables from the 1998 edition) and 5 new figures demonstrating sprinkler configuration in accordance with the tables. The tables addressed palletized and solid pile storage, and rack storage, of Level 2 and Level 3, cartoned and uncartoned, aerosol products. New sections on damage-limiting construction, fume incinerators, shrink-wrapping of aerosol products, and special protection design were added. NFPA 30B was also reformatted to conform to the *Manual of Style for NFPA Technical Committee Documents* requirements, including reorganization and renumbering of chapters, elimination of exceptions, deletion of nonenforceable language, and clarification of mandatory requirements.

The 2007 edition of NFPA 30B clarified the requirements for aisle widths in storage facilities.

In the 2010 edition of NFPA 30B, the Committee revised the definition of aerosol container to reflect the new requirements from DOT that allow the use of plastic aerosol containers up to a maximum size of 1000 ml (33.8 fl oz). The revised definition of aerosol container prompted changes in several locations of the code to accommodate aerosol products in plastic containers. In support of the revised definition of aerosol container, the Committee also added new material in Annex B that provided several sets of fire test data on the results of testing aerosols in plastic containers.

Technical Committee on Aerosol Products

Peter J. Willse, Chair
XL Global Asset Protection Services, CT [I]

Gerald J. Basta, Global Risk Consultants Corporation, IL [SE]
Tracey D. Bellamy, Telgian Corporation, GA [U]
  Rep. The Home Depot
James A. Bloome, Packaging Technologies, Inc., IA [M]
Richard A. Familia, Giant Resource Recovery Company, SC [U]
William A. Frauenheim, III, Diversified CPC International, Inc., IL [M]
  Rep. Consumer Specialty Products Association
David L. Fredrickson, Fredrickson & Associates LLC, WI [SE]
Edward S. Goldhammer, Aon/Schirmer Engineering Corporation, NV [I]
David Grandaw, Kidde-Fenwal, Inc., IL [M]
James Koskan, SUPERVALU, Inc., MN [U]
John A. LeBlanc, FM Global, MA [I]
David J. LeBlanc, Tyco Fire Suppression & Building Products, RI [M]
  Rep. National Fire Sprinkler Association

Michael J. Madden, Hughes Associates, Inc., CA [SE]
Michael J. Nappi, Potomac Electric Power Company, DC [U]
  Rep. Edison Electric Institute
Martin J. Pabich, Underwriters Laboratories Inc., IL [RT]
Donald E. Rowson, Industrial Hydrocarbons, Inc., CA [SE]
George A. Seuss, Jr., The Hanover Insurance Group, MD [I]
David C. Tabar, The Sherwin-Williams Company, OH [M]
Tim N. Testerman, Procter & Gamble Company, OH [M]
  Rep. NFPA Industrial Fire Protection Section
Jack W. Thacker, Allan Automatic Sprinkler Corp. of So. California, CA [IM]
  Rep. National Fire Sprinkler Association
Daniel J. Venier, Wells Fargo Insurance Services, MI [I]

Alternates

Thomas B. Arch, Global Risk Consultants Corporation, MN [SE]
  (Alt. to G. J. Basta)
Emre Ergun, Kidde-Fenwal, Inc., MA [M]
  (Alt. to D. Grandaw)
D. Douglas Fratz, Consumer Specialty Products Association, DC [M]
  (Alt. to W. A. Frauenheim, III)
Pravinray D. Gandhi, Underwriters Laboratories Inc., IL [RT]
  (Alt. to M. J. Pabich)
Kenneth E. Isman, National Fire Sprinkler Association, Inc., NY [IM]
  (Alt. to J. W. Thacker)

Jeffrey C. Koehn, Hanover Specialty Property, MD [I]
  (Alt. to G. A. Seuss, Jr.)
Ronald A. Schulz, XL Global Asset Protection Services, MI [I]
  (Alt. to P. J. Willse)
David C. Swenson, The Sherwin-Williams Company, OH [M]
  (Alt. to D. C. Tabar)
Paul A. Wolf, Packaging Technologies Inc., IA [M]
  (Alt. to J. A. Bloome)
Martin H. Workman, The Viking Corporation, MI [M]
  (Alt. to D. J. LeBlanc)

Martha H. Curtis, NFPA Staff Liaison

This list represents the membership at the time the Committee was balloted on the final text of this edition. Since that time, changes in the membership may have occurred. A key to classifications is found at the back of the document.

NOTE: Membership on a committee shall not in and of itself constitute an endorsement of the Association or any document developed by the committee on which the member serves.

Committee Scope: This Committee shall have primary responsibility for documents on safeguarding against the fire and explosion hazards associated with the manufacturing, handling, and storage of aerosol products.

Contents

Chapter 1	**Administration**	**30B– 4**
1.1	Scope	30B– 4
1.2	Purpose	30B– 4
1.3	Application	30B– 4
1.4	Retroactivity	30B– 4
1.5	Equivalency	30B– 4
1.6	Enforcement	30B– 4
1.7	Classification of Aerosol Products in Metal Containers and Plastic or Glass Containers Less Than or Equal to 118 ml (4 fl oz).	30B– 4
1.8	Marking of Packages of Aerosol Products	30B– 5
Chapter 2	**Referenced Publications**	**30B– 5**
2.1	General	30B– 5
2.2	NFPA Publications	30B– 5
2.3	Other Publications	30B– 5
2.4	References for Extracts in Mandatory Sections	30B– 5
Chapter 3	**Definitions**	**30B– 6**
3.1	General	30B– 6
3.2	NFPA Official Definitions	30B– 6
3.3	General Definitions	30B– 6
3.4	Definitions Specific to Chapter 5	30B– 8
Chapter 4	**Basic Requirements**	**30B– 8**
4.1	Site Requirements	30B– 8
4.2	Building Construction	30B– 8
4.3	Electrical Installations	30B– 8
4.4	Heating Equipment	30B– 8
4.5	Flammable Liquids and Gases	30B– 8
4.6	Fire Protection	30B– 8
4.7	Fire Alarms	30B– 9
4.8	Sources of Ignition	30B– 9
Chapter 5	**Manufacturing Facilities**	**30B– 9**
5.1	Scope	30B– 9
5.2	Basic Requirements	30B– 9
5.3	Building Construction	30B– 9
5.4	Ventilation	30B–10
5.5	Electrical Equipment	30B–11
5.6	Control of Static Electricity	30B–11
5.7	Combustible Gas Detection Systems	30B–11
5.8	Automatic Sprinkler Protection	30B–11
5.9	Fixed Extinguishing Systems	30B–11
5.10	Spill Control	30B–11
5.11	Deflagration Suppression Systems	30B–11
5.12	Equipment Interlocks	30B–11
5.13	Process Operating Requirements	30B–11
5.14	Shrink-Wrapping of Aerosol Products	30B–13
5.15	Aerosol Product Laboratories	30B–13
Chapter 6	**Storage in Warehouses and Storage Areas**	**30B–13**
6.1	Basic Requirements	30B–13
6.2	Storage of Level 1 Aerosol Products	30B–13
6.3	Storage of Level 2 and Level 3 Aerosol Products	30B–13
Chapter 7	**Mercantile Occupancies**	**30B–32**
7.1	Sales Display Areas — Aerosol Storage Not Exceeding 2.4 m (8 ft) High	30B–32
7.2	Sales Display Areas — Aerosol Storage Exceeding 2.4 m (8 ft) High	30B–32
7.3	Back Stock Storage Areas	30B–33
7.4	Special Protection Design	30B–33
Chapter 8	**Operations and Maintenance**	**30B–34**
8.1	Means of Egress	30B–34
8.2	Powered Industrial Trucks	30B–34
8.3	Control of Ignition Sources	30B–34
8.4	Aisles	30B–35
8.5	Waste Disposal	30B–35
8.6	Inspection and Maintenance	30B–35
8.7	Static Electricity	30B–35
Annex A	**Explanatory Material**	**30B–35**
Annex B	**Mechanism of Fire Growth in Aerosol Containers**	**30B–41**
Annex C	**Determining the Classification Level of Aerosol Products in Metal Containers**	**30B–52**
Annex D	**Flammability Labeling of Aerosol Products**	**30B–52**
Annex E	**Loss Experience**	**30B–52**
Annex F	**Chemical Heat of Combustion**	**30B–53**
Annex G	**Sample Ordinance Adopting NFPA 30B**	**30B–57**
Annex H	**Informational References**	**30B–58**
Index		**30B–59**

2011 Edition

NFPA 30B

Code for the

Manufacture and Storage of Aerosol Products

2011 Edition

***IMPORTANT NOTE:** This NFPA document is made available for use subject to important notices and legal disclaimers. These notices and disclaimers appear in all publications containing this document and may be found under the heading "Important Notices and Disclaimers Concerning NFPA Documents." They can also be obtained on request from NFPA or viewed at www.nfpa.org/disclaimers.*

NOTICE: An asterisk (*) following the number or letter designating a paragraph indicates that explanatory material on the paragraph can be found in Annex A.

Changes other than editorial are indicated by a vertical rule beside the paragraph, table, or figure in which the change occurred. These rules are included as an aid to the user in identifying changes from the previous edition. Where one or more complete paragraphs have been deleted, the deletion is indicated by a bullet (•) between the paragraphs that remain.

A reference in brackets [ ] following a section or paragraph indicates material that has been extracted from another NFPA document. As an aid to the user, the complete title and edition of the source documents for extracts in mandatory sections of the document are given in Chapter 2 and those for extracts in informational sections are given in Annex H. Extracted text may be edited for consistency and style and may include the revision of internal paragraph references and other references as appropriate. Requests for interpretations or revisions of extracted text shall be sent to the technical committee responsible for the source document.

Information on referenced publications can be found in Chapter 2 and Annex H.

Chapter 1   Administration

1.1 Scope.

1.1.1 This code shall apply to the manufacture, storage, and display of aerosol products as herein defined.

1.1.2* This code shall not apply to the storage and display of containers whose contents are comprised entirely of LP-Gas products.

1.1.3 This code shall not apply to post-consumer processing of aerosol containers.

1.1.4* This code shall not apply to containers that do not meet the definition of *Aerosol Container* (*see 3.3.2*).

1.1.4.1 Metal containers that contain a product that meets the definitions in 3.3.1 and 3.3.3, but are larger than 1000 ml (33.8 fl oz) shall not be classified as aerosol products, and this code shall not apply to the manufacture, storage, and display of such containers.

1.2* Purpose. The purpose of this code is to provide minimum requirements for the prevention and control of fires and explosions in facilities that manufacture, store, or display aerosol products.

1.3 Application.

1.3.1 Chapters 4, 5, and 8 shall apply to facilities or portions of facilities that manufacture aerosol products, including gas-filling, product-filling, and packaging operations.

1.3.2 Chapters 4, 6, and 8 shall apply to facilities or portions of facilities that store aerosol products, such as storage areas, storage rooms, and warehouses.

1.3.3 Chapters 4, 7, and 8 shall apply to the storage and display of aerosol products in mercantile occupancies.

1.4* Retroactivity.

1.4.1 The provisions of this code are considered necessary to provide a reasonable level of protection from loss of life and property from fire and explosion. They reflect situations and the state of the art at the time the code was issued.

1.4.2 Unless otherwise noted, it is not intended that the provisions of this code be applied to facilities, equipment, structures, or installations that were existing or approved for construction or installation prior to the effective date of the code, except in those cases where it is determined by the authority having jurisdiction that the existing situation involves a distinct hazard to life or adjacent property.

1.5 Equivalency. Nothing in this code is intended to prevent the use of systems, methods, or devices of equivalent or superior quality, strength, fire resistance, effectiveness, durability, and safety over those prescribed by this code, provided technical documentation is submitted to the authority having jurisdiction to demonstrate equivalency, and the system, method, or device is approved for the intended purpose.

1.6 Enforcement. This code shall be administered and enforced by the authority having jurisdiction designated by the governing authority. (*See Annex G for sample wording for enabling legislation.*)

1.7* Classification of Aerosol Products in Metal Containers and Plastic or Glass Containers Less Than or Equal to 118 ml (4 fl oz). See Annex C.

1.7.1 Aerosol products shall be classified by means of the calculation of their chemical or theoretical heats of combustion and shall be designated Level 1, Level 2, or Level 3 in accordance with 1.7.2 through 1.7.4 and Table 1.7.1.

1.7.1.1 In lieu of classification by means of the chemical heats of combustion, aerosol products shall be permitted to be classified by means of data obtained from properly conducted full-scale fire tests that utilize a 12-pallet test array.

Table 1.7.1 Aerosol Classification

\>	≤	Aerosol Classification Level
\multicolumn{2}{l|}{If the chemical heat of combustion is}	
0	20 kJ/g (8,600 Btu/lb)	1
20 kJ/g (8,600 Btu/lb)	30 kJ/g (13,000 Btu/lb)	2
30 kJ/g (13,000 Btu/lb)	—	3

1.7.1.2 The fire tests shall be conducted at an approved testing laboratory. *(See Annex C for information on the 12-pallet test array.)*

1.7.2 Level 1 Aerosol Products. Level 1 aerosol products are those with a total chemical heat of combustion that is less than or equal to 20 kJ/g (8600 Btu/lb).

1.7.3 Level 2 Aerosol Products. Level 2 aerosol products are those with a total chemical heat of combustion that is greater than 20 kJ/g (8600 Btu/lb), but less than or equal to 30 kJ/g (13,000 Btu/lb).

1.7.4 Level 3 Aerosol Products. Level 3 aerosol products are those with a total chemical heat of combustion that is greater than 30 kJ/g (13,000 Btu/lb).

1.8 Marking of Packages of Aerosol Products.

1.8.1 Manufacturers of aerosol products shall ensure that all cartons or packages of aerosol products are identified on at least one exterior side with the classification of the aerosol products contained therein, in accordance with Section 1.7.

1.8.2 Cartons or packages containing aerosol products in metal containers or glass and plastic containers 118 ml (4 fl oz) or less shall be clearly marked as follows:

Level _____ Aerosols

1.8.3 Cartons or packages containing plastic aerosol containers greater than 118 ml (4 fl oz) shall be clearly marked on the exterior of the carton as follows:

Plastic Aerosol Container

Chapter 2   Referenced Publications

2.1 General. The documents or portions thereof listed in this chapter are referenced within this code and shall be considered part of the requirements of this document.

2.2 NFPA Publications. National Fire Protection Association, 1 Batterymarch Park, Quincy, MA 02169-7471.

NFPA 1, *Fire Code,* 2009 edition.
NFPA 10, *Standard for Portable Fire Extinguishers,* 2010 edition.
NFPA 11, *Standard for Low-, Medium-, and High-Expansion Foam,* 2010 edition.
NFPA 12, *Standard on Carbon Dioxide Extinguishing Systems,* 2008 edition.
NFPA 12A, *Standard on Halon 1301 Fire Extinguishing Systems,* 2009 edition.
NFPA 13, *Standard for the Installation of Sprinkler Systems,* 2010 edition.
NFPA 14, *Standard for the Installation of Standpipe and Hose Systems,* 2010 edition.
NFPA 16, *Standard for the Installation of Foam-Water Sprinkler and Foam-Water Spray Systems,* 2007 edition.
NFPA 17, *Standard for Dry Chemical Extinguishing Systems,* 2009 edition.
NFPA 20, *Standard for the Installation of Stationary Pumps for Fire Protection,* 2010 edition.
NFPA 22, *Standard for Water Tanks for Private Fire Protection,* 2008 edition.
NFPA 24, *Standard for the Installation of Private Fire Service Mains and Their Appurtenances,* 2010 edition.
NFPA 30, *Flammable and Combustible Liquids Code,* 2008 edition.
NFPA 31, *Standard for the Installation of Oil-Burning Equipment,* 2006 edition.
NFPA 45, *Standard on Fire Protection for Laboratories Using Chemicals,* 2011 edition.
NFPA 54, *National Fuel Gas Code,* 2009 edition.
NFPA 58, *Liquefied Petroleum Gas Code,* 2011 edition.
NFPA 68, *Standard on Explosion Protection by Deflagration Venting,* 2007 edition.
NFPA 69, *Standard on Explosion Prevention Systems,* 2008 edition.
NFPA 70®, *National Electrical Code®,* 2011 edition.
NFPA 72®, *National Fire Alarm and Signaling Code,* 2010 edition.
NFPA 80, *Standard for Fire Doors and Other Opening Protectives,* 2010 edition.
NFPA 85, *Boiler and Combustion Systems Hazards Code,* 2007 edition.
NFPA 86, *Standard for Ovens and Furnaces,* 2011 edition.
NFPA 90A, *Standard for the Installation of Air-Conditioning and Ventilating Systems,* 2009 edition.
NFPA 101®, *Life Safety Code®,* 2009 edition.
NFPA 505, *Fire Safety Standard for Powered Industrial Trucks Including Type Designations, Areas of Use, Conversions, Maintenance, and Operations,* 2011 edition.
NFPA 2001, *Standard on Clean Agent Fire Extinguishing Systems,* 2008 edition.

2.3 Other Publications.

2.3.1 ANSI Publication. American National Standards Institute, Inc., 25 West 43rd Street, 4th Floor, New York, NY 10036.

ANSI/ASME B56.1, *Safety Standard for Low-Lift and High-Lift Trucks,* 2004.

2.3.2 ASTM Publications. ASTM International, 100 Barr Harbor Drive, P.O. Box C700, West Conshohocken, PA 19428-2959.

ASTM A 47/A 47M, *Standard Specification for Ferritic Malleable Iron Castings,* 2004.

ASTM A 48/A 48M, *Standard Specification for Gray Iron Castings,* 2008.

ASTM A 395/A 395M, *Standard Specification for Ferritic Ductile Iron Pressure-Retaining Castings for Use at Elevated Temperatures,* 2004.

ASTM A 536-84 (e1), *Standard Specification for Ductile Iron Castings,* 2004.

ASTM D 323, *Standard Test Method for Vapor Pressure of Petroleum Products (Reid Method),* 2006.

2.3.3 Other Publications. *Merriam-Webster's Collegiate Dictionary,* 11th edition, Merriam-Webster, Inc., Springfield, MA, 2003.

2.4 References for Extracts in Mandatory Sections.
NFPA 1, *Fire Code,* 2009 edition.
NFPA 13, *Standard for the Installation of Sprinkler Systems,* 2010 edition.
NFPA 30, *Flammable and Combustible Liquids Code,* 2008 edition.
NFPA 68, *Standard on Explosion Protection by Deflagration Venting,* 2007 edition.
NFPA 72®, *National Fire Alarm and Signaling Code,* 2010 edition.
NFPA 77, *Recommended Practice on Static Electricity,* 2007 edition.
NFPA 5000®, *Building Construction and Safety Code®,* 2009 edition.

Chapter 3 Definitions

3.1 General. The definitions contained in this chapter shall apply to the terms used in this code. Where terms are not defined in this chapter or within another chapter, they shall be defined using their ordinarily accepted meanings within the context in which they are used. *Merriam-Webster's Collegiate Dictionary*, 11th edition, shall be the source for the ordinarily accepted meaning.

3.2 NFPA Official Definitions.

3.2.1* Approved. Acceptable to the authority having jurisdiction.

3.2.2* Authority Having Jurisdiction (AHJ). An organization, office, or individual responsible for enforcing the requirements of a code or standard, or for approving equipment, materials, an installation, or a procedure.

3.2.3* Code. A standard that is an extensive compilation of provisions covering broad subject matter or that is suitable for adoption into law independently of other codes and standards.

3.2.4 Shall. Indicates a mandatory requirement.

3.2.5 Should. Indicates a recommendation or that which is advised but not required.

3.3 General Definitions.

3.3.1* Aerosol. A product that is dispensed from an aerosol container by a propellant.

3.3.2* Aerosol Container. A metal can or plastic container, up to a maximum size of 1000 ml (33.8 fl oz), or a glass or plastic bottle, up to a maximum size of 118 ml (4 fl oz), that is designed and intended to dispense an aerosol.

3.3.3* Aerosol Propellant. The liquefied or compressed gas that expels the contents from an aerosol container when the valve is actuated. A propellant is considered flammable if it forms a flammable mixture with air or if a flame is self-propagating in a mixture of the propellant and air.

3.3.4 Back Stock Area. The area of a mercantile occupancy that is physically separated from the sales area and not intended to be accessible to the public.

3.3.5* Base Product (Concentrate). The contents of an aerosol container, excluding the propellant.

3.3.6 Basement. For the purposes of this code, a story of a building or structure having one-half or more of its height below ground level and to which access for fire-fighting purposes is restricted. [**30,** 2008]

3.3.7 Bonding. For the purpose of controlling static electric hazards, the process of connecting two or more conductive objects together by means of a conductor so that they are at the same electrical potential, but not necessarily at the same potential as the earth. [**77,** 2007]

3.3.8 Carton. A cardboard or fiberboard box that encloses a product.

3.3.9* Cold Filling. The pressurizing of an aerosol container by cooling the propellant (and sometimes the product) below its boiling point and transferring it into the aerosol container before the valve is put in place. The operation is usually carried out at atmospheric pressure (that is, high pressure is not needed).

3.3.10 Combustion Efficiency. The ratio of chemical heat of combustion to theoretical heat of combustion.

3.3.11 Damage-Limiting Construction. For the purposes of this code, any set of construction elements, used individually or in combination, which will act to limit damage from an explosion, including open structures, pressure relieving construction, or pressure resistant construction. [**30,** 2008]

3.3.12 Encapsulation. A method of packaging consisting of a plastic sheet completely enclosing the sides and top of a pallet load containing a combustible commodity or a combustible package or a group of combustible commodities or combustible packages. Combustible commodities individually wrapped in plastic sheeting and stored exposed in a pallet load also are to be considered encapsulated. Totally noncombustible commodities on wood pallets enclosed only by a plastic sheet as described are not covered under this definition. Banding (i.e., stretch-wrapping around the sides only of a pallet load) is not considered to be encapsulation. Where there are holes or voids in the plastic or waterproof cover on the top of the carton that exceed more than half the area of the cover, the term *encapsulated* does not apply. The term *encapsulated* does not apply to plastic-enclosed products or packages inside a large, nonplastic, enclosed container. [**13,** 2010]

3.3.13 Fire Area. An area of a building separated from the remainder of the building by construction having a fire resistance of at least 1 hour and having all communicating openings properly protected by an assembly having a fire resistance rating of at least 1 hour. [**30,** 2008]

3.3.14 Flammable Propellant. See 3.3.3, Aerosol Propellant.

3.3.15 Grounding. The process of bonding one or more conductive objects to the ground, so that all objects are at zero (0) electrical potential; also referred to as earthing. [**77,** 2007]

3.3.16 Heat of Combustion.

3.3.16.1 *Chemical Heat of Combustion (H_c).* The amount of heat released, in kJ/g (Btu/lb), when a substance is oxidized to yield stable end products, including water as a vapor, as measured under actual fire conditions in a normal ambient (air) atmosphere.

3.3.16.2 *Theoretical Heat of Combustion.* The amount of heat released, in kJ/g (Btu/lb), when a substance is completely oxidized to yield stable end products, including water as a vapor, as measured using an oxygen bomb calorimeter. Alternatively, the theoretical heat of combustion can be calculated from heat of formation data, heat of combustion data, or molecular calculation data as reported in the literature and assuming all products are in the vapor state.

3.3.17 Horizontal Barrier. A solid barrier in the horizontal position covering the entire rack, including all flue spaces at certain height increments, to prevent vertical fire spread. [**13,** 2010]

3.3.18 Inside Liquid Storage Area. A room or building used for the storage of liquids in containers or portable tanks, separated from other occupancies. [**30,** 2008]

3.3.19 (Liquid Storage) Control Area. A building or portion of a building within which flammable and combustible liquids are allowed to be stored, dispensed, and used or handled in quantities that do not exceed the maximum allowable quantity (MAQ) as established by NFPA 30. [**30,** 2008]

3.3.20 Liquid Storage Room. A room that is used for the storage of liquids in containers, portable tanks, or intermediate bulk containers, has a floor area that does not exceed 46.5 m² (500 ft²), and might be totally enclosed within a building — that is, the room might have no exterior walls. [30, 2008]

3.3.21 Liquid Warehouse. A separate, detached building or an attached building that is used for warehousing-type operations for liquids and whose exterior wall comprises at least 25 percent of the building perimeter. [30, 2008]

3.3.22 Liquids.

3.3.22.1* *Combustible Liquid.* Any liquid that has a closed-cup flash point at or above 100°F (37.8°C), as determined by the test procedures and apparatus set forth in Section 4.4 of NFPA 30, *Flammable and Combustible Liquids Code.* [30, 2008]

3.3.22.2* *Flammable Liquid.* Any liquid that has a closed-cup flash point below 100°F (37.8°C), as determined by the test procedures and apparatus set forth in Section 4.4 of NFPA 30, *Flammable and Combustible Liquids Code*, and a Reid vapor pressure that does not exceed an absolute pressure of 40 psi (276 kPa) at 100°F (37.8°C), as determined by ASTM D 323, *Standard Test Method for Vapor Pressure of Petroleum Products (Reid Method).* [30, 2008]

3.3.22.3 *Unstable Liquid.* A liquid that, in the pure state or as commercially produced or transported, will vigorously polymerize, decompose, undergo condensation reaction, or become self-reactive under conditions of shock, pressure, or temperature. [30, 2008]

3.3.23 Mercantile Occupancy. An occupancy used for the display and sale of merchandise. [5000, 2009]

3.3.24* Net Weight. Total weight of base product and propellant as indicated on aerosol container label.

3.3.25 Noncommunicating Wall. The shared portion of a wall between two building areas having no openings.

3.3.26 Packaging Types.

3.3.26.1 *Packaging Type — Cartoned.* Aerosol cans packaged in at least a single layer of corrugated cardboard. The cardboard must cover at least the top, bottom, and two complete sides of the unit. The two other sides must be at least 60 percent covered.

3.3.26.2 *Packaging Type — Display Cut.* Aerosol cans packaged in at least a single layer of corrugated cardboard where the top and parts of the face and sides of the carton have been removed for retail sales.

3.3.26.3 *Packaging Type — Uncartoned.* Aerosol cans arranged on slip sheets or trays shrink-wrapped together in packs on a pallet or packaging that does not meet the definition of cartoned.

3.3.27 Protection for Exposures. Fire protection for structures on property adjacent to an aerosol product manufacturing or storage facility. Fire protection for such structures shall be acceptable where located either within the jurisdiction of any public fire department or adjacent to plants having private fire brigades capable of providing cooling water streams on the adjacent property.

3.3.28* Rack. Any combination of vertical, horizontal, and diagonal members that supports stored materials. [1, 2009]

3.3.28.1 *Open Rack.* Racks without shelving or with shelving in racks that are fixed in place with shelves having a solid surface and a shelf area equal to or less than 20 ft² (1.9 m²) or with shelves having a wire mesh, slatted surface, or other material with openings representing at least 50 percent of the shelf area including the horizontal area of rack members and where the flue spaces are maintained. [13, 2010]

3.3.28.2 *Rack Shelf Area.* The area of the horizontal surface of a shelf in a rack defined by perimeter aisle(s) or minimum 6 in. (152 mm) flue spaces on all four sides, or by the placement of loads that block openings that would otherwise serve as the required flue spaces. [13, 2010]

3.3.28.3 *Slatted Shelf Rack.* A rack where shelves are fixed in place with a series of narrow individual solid supports used as the shelf material and spaced apart with regular openings. [13, 2010]

3.3.28.4 *Solid Shelf Rack.* A rack where shelves are fixed in place with a solid, slatted, or wire mesh barrier used as the shelf material and having limited openings in the shelf area. [13, 2010]

3.3.29 Sales Display Area. The area of a mercantile occupancy that is open to the public for the purpose of viewing and purchasing goods, wares, and merchandise. Individuals are free to circulate among the items, which are typically displayed on shelves, on racks, or on the floor.

3.3.30 Separate Inside Storage Area. A room or building used for the storage of aerosol products and separated from other occupancies.

3.3.30.1 *Separate Inside Storage Area — Attached Building.* A building that has only one common wall with a building that has other occupancies.

3.3.30.2 *Separate Inside Storage Area — Cut-Off Room.* A room within a building that has at least one exterior wall.

3.3.30.3 *Separate Inside Storage Area — Fenced Enclosure.* A segregated area meeting the requirements of 6.3.5.3.2.

3.3.30.4 *Separate Inside Storage Area — Inside Room.* A room totally enclosed within a building and having no exterior walls.

3.3.31 Sprinklers.

3.3.31.1 *Early Suppression Fast-Response (ESFR) Sprinklers.* A type of fast-response sprinkler listed for its capability to provide fire suppression of specific high-challenge fire hazards.

3.3.31.2* *Face Sprinklers.* Standard sprinklers located in transverse flue spaces along the aisle or in the rack, within 0.46 m (1½ ft) of the aisle face of storage and used to oppose vertical development of fire on the external face of storage.

3.3.32 Warehouse.

3.3.32.1 *Aerosol Warehouse.* A detached building or a separate portion of a building used for the storage, shipping, and receiving of aerosol products.

3.3.32.2 *General-Purpose Warehouse.* A detached building or a separate portion of a building used only for the storage, shipping, and receiving of mixed commodities.

3.3.32.3 *Liquid Warehouse.* A separate, detached building or an attached building that is used for warehousing-type operations for liquids and whose exterior wall comprises at least 25 percent of the building perimeter. [30, 2008]

3.4 Definitions Specific to Chapter 5.

3.4.1 Base Product Filler (Concentrate Filler). A machine used to fill the aerosol container with the base product prior to addition of the propellant.

3.4.2* Button Tipper (Actuator Placer). The machine that places the valve actuator (spray tip) onto the aerosol container after the base product has been added.

3.4.3 Fume Incinerator. Any separate or independent combustion equipment or device that entrains the process exhaust for the purpose of direct thermal or catalytic destruction, which can include heat recovery.

3.4.4 Local Ventilation. A ventilation system whose exhaust inlet is located close to the point of vapor release so as to remove the vapor from the point of release.

3.4.5 Propellant Charging Pump (Charging Pump). A pump used to boost the liquid propellant to the pressure required by the propellant filler, usually 2070 to 8280 kPa (300 to 1200 psi). Tank farm transfer pumps normally supply the suction side of the propellant charging pump at pressures of 100 to 690 kPa (15 to 100 psi) above the propellant's vapor pressure.

3.4.6* Propellant Charging Room (Gas House, Gassing Room). Any room or enclosure in which the propellant is added to the aerosol containers. The definition includes prefabricated gas houses and enclosures.

3.4.7* Propellant Filler (Gasser, Propellant Charger). A machine that adds the propellant to the aerosol container.

3.4.8 Pump Room. A room or enclosure outside the propellant charging rooms in which flammable propellant charging pumps and, in some cases, vacuum pumps are located.

3.4.9 Radiant Energy-Sensing Fire Detector. A device that detects radiant energy, such as ultraviolet, visible, or infrared, that is emitted as a product of combustion reaction and obeys the laws of optics. [*72*, 2010]

3.4.10 Reject Container Receptacle. A receptacle used to store scrap, partially filled, or fully filled aerosol containers prior to disposal.

3.4.11* Test Bath (Hot Tank, Water Bath). A water tank in which pressurized aerosol containers are tested to verify the container strength and to detect leaks by immersion in water.

3.4.12 Vacuum Pump. A pump used to evacuate the head space (above the base product) of an aerosol container prior to addition of the propellant.

3.4.13 Valve Crimper (Crimper). A machine that seals the valve cup or valve ferrule to the aerosol container.

Chapter 4 Basic Requirements

4.1 Site Requirements. Distances between buildings used for the manufacture or storage of aerosol products and adjacent buildings or property lines that are or can be built upon shall be based on sound engineering principles.

4.2 Building Construction.

4.2.1 Openings in fire walls or fire barriers shall be kept to a minimum.

4.2.1.1 All openings (i.e., personnel doorways, ductwork, conveyor line, etc.) shall be protected with automatic-closing or self-closing fire doors or dampers.

4.2.1.2 Fire doors shall be installed in accordance with NFPA 80, *Standard for Fire Doors and Other Opening Protectives*.

4.2.1.3 Fire dampers shall be installed in accordance with manufacturer's instructions and NFPA 90A, *Standard for the Installation of Air-Conditioning and Ventilating Systems*.

4.2.2 Means of Egress.

4.2.2.1 Means of egress shall comply with applicable provisions of NFPA *101, Life Safety Code*.

4.2.2.2 The design and construction of conveyor lines and other physical obstacles, such as in the flammable propellant charging and pump rooms, shall not allow entrapment of personnel and shall provide for direct access to exits.

4.3 Electrical Installations.

4.3.1 All electrical equipment and wiring, including heating equipment, shall be installed in accordance with *NFPA 70, National Electrical Code*.

4.3.1.1 Electrical equipment and wiring in areas where flammable liquids or flammable gases are handled shall meet the additional requirements of Articles 500 and 501 of *NFPA 70, National Electrical Code*.

4.3.2 Aerosol product storage and display areas shall be considered unclassified for purposes of electrical installation.

4.4 Heating Equipment. Heating equipment shall be installed in accordance with the applicable requirements of the following:

(1) NFPA 31, *Standard for the Installation of Oil-Burning Equipment*
(2) NFPA 54, *National Fuel Gas Code*
(3) NFPA 58, *Liquefied Petroleum Gas Code*
(4) NFPA 85, *Boiler and Combustion Systems Hazards Code*

4.5 Flammable Liquids and Gases. Areas in which flammable liquids and flammable gases are handled or stored shall meet the applicable requirements of the following:

(1) NFPA 30, *Flammable and Combustible Liquids Code*
(2) NFPA 58, *Liquefied Petroleum Gas Code*

4.6 Fire Protection.

4.6.1 Automatic Sprinkler Protection. Installations of automatic sprinklers, where required by this code, shall be installed in accordance with NFPA 13, *Standard for the Installation of Sprinkler Systems*, and the provisions of this code.

4.6.1.1 Where the provisions of this code and NFPA 13, *Standard for the Installation of Sprinkler Systems*, differ, the provisions of this code shall prevail.

4.6.1.2 Where this code does not address specific automatic sprinkler protection criteria, the provisions of NFPA 13, *Standard for the Installation of Sprinkler Systems*, shall prevail.

4.6.2 Standpipe and Hose System. Installations of standpipe and hose systems, where required by this code, shall be designed and installed in accordance with NFPA 14, *Standard for the Installation of Standpipe and Hose Systems*, and with the provisions of this code. Only combination or spray hose nozzles shall be used.

4.6.3 Portable Fire Extinguishers. Fire extinguishers shall be provided in accordance with NFPA 10, *Standard for Portable Fire Extinguishers*.

4.6.4 Water Supplies.

4.6.4.1 In addition to the water supply requirements for automatic sprinkler systems, a minimum requirement for hose stream supply for combined inside and outside hose streams shall be provided in accordance with one of the following:

(1) 1900 L/min (500 gpm) for buildings protected with spray and/or large drop sprinkler protection
(2) 950 L/min (250 gpm) for buildings protected with ESFR sprinkler protection
(3) 3800 L/min (1000 gpm) for buildings without automatic sprinkler protection

4.6.4.1.1 The water supply shall be sufficient to provide the required hose stream demand for a minimum duration of 2 hours, unless otherwise specified in 6.3.2.

4.6.4.1.2 The water supply system shall be designed and installed in accordance with NFPA 24, *Standard for the Installation of Private Fire Service Mains and Their Appurtenances*.

4.6.4.1.3 The water supply requirements shall be permitted as modified by the provisions of this code.

4.6.4.2 Installations of fire pumps and tanks that are needed to supply the required fire protection water shall be installed in accordance with NFPA 20, *Standard for the Installation of Stationary Pumps for Fire Protection*, and NFPA 22, *Standard for Water Tanks for Private Fire Protection*.

4.7 Fire Alarms. Fire alarm systems shall be installed, tested, and maintained in accordance with applicable requirements of *NFPA 72, National Fire Alarm and Signaling Code*.

4.8 Sources of Ignition.

4.8.1 In areas where flammable gases or flammable vapors might be present, precautions shall be taken to prevent ignition by eliminating or controlling sources of ignition.

4.8.2 Sources of ignition shall include, but are not limited to, the following:

(1) Open flames
(2) Lightning
(3) Hot surfaces
(4) Radiant heat
(5) Smoking
(6) Cutting and welding
(7) Spontaneous ignition
(8) Frictional heat or sparks
(9) Static electricity
(10) Electrical arcs and sparks
(11) Stray currents
(12) Ovens, furnaces, and other heating equipment
(13) Automotive vehicles
(14) Material-handling equipment

Chapter 5 Manufacturing Facilities

5.1* Scope. This chapter shall apply to the manufacture of aerosol products containing flammable or combustible base product or a flammable propellant.

5.2 Basic Requirements.

5.2.1 Manufacturing buildings shall be located at least 8 m (25 ft) from the nearest property line that is or can be built upon.

5.2.2 Flammable propellant storage tanks shall be located in accordance with the provisions of NFPA 58, *Liquefied Petroleum Gas Code*.

5.2.3 Flammable and combustible liquids shall be stored in accordance with the provisions of NFPA 30, *Flammable and Combustible Liquids Code*.

5.2.4 Separation of Flammable Propellant Charging and Pump Rooms.

5.2.4.1 Flammable propellant charging and pump rooms shall be separated from adjacent buildings or structures by noncommunicating walls or by a distance of at least 1.5 m (5 ft), and from inside areas by noncommunicating walls.

5.2.4.1.1 Noncommunicating walls shall have a minimum fire resistance rating of 1 hour.

5.2.4.1.2 Noncommunicating walls shall meet the requirements of 5.3.4.

5.2.4.2 Flammable propellant charging and pump rooms shall be separated from flammable propellant storage tanks and from flammable and combustible liquids storage by a distance of at least 8 m (25 ft).

5.3* Building Construction.

5.3.1 Buildings or structures involved in the manufacturing of aerosol products shall have no basement or any space below the finish floor of the ground level.

5.3.1.1 Subject to the approval of the authority having jurisdiction, buildings or structures shall be permitted to have basements or below-ground level areas provided they are ventilated at a minimum flow rate of 0.3 m^3/min·m^2 (1 ft^3/min·ft^2) of floor area and provided the nearest entrance or access point is located at least 15.1 m (50 ft) in any direction from the nearest point of the gas house.

5.3.2 Flammable propellant charging operations shall be limited to the ground floor.

5.3.3 Flammable propellant charging and pump rooms shall be classified as High Hazard Areas, as defined by NFPA *101, Life Safety Code*.

5.3.4 Damage-Limiting Construction.

5.3.4.1* New flammable propellant charging rooms, flammable propellant pump rooms, and rooms in which Class IA liquids or unstable liquids are handled shall be designed to direct flame, combustion gases, and pressures resulting from deflagration away from important buildings or occupied areas through the use of damage-limiting construction.

5.3.4.1.1 The damage-limiting construction shall be in accordance with recognized standards and shall be subject to approval of the authority having jurisdiction.

5.3.4.1.2 Existing rooms that cannot be designed to direct flame, combustion gases, and pressures resulting from a deflagration away from important buildings or other occupied areas shall be designed to control the deflagration to the room of origin using techniques provided in NFPA 69, *Standard on Explosion Prevention Systems*.

5.3.4.2 The walls, roof, and all structural members shall be designed to withstand a static pressure of at least five times the release pressure of the deflagration vent closure, but in no case less than 4.8 kPa (100 lb/ft^2).

5.3.4.3 Damage-limiting construction shall be designed in accordance with NFPA 68, *Standard on Explosion Protection by Deflagration Venting*.

5.3.4.4 Walls, floors, ceilings, or roofs of flammable propellant charging and pump rooms not used for deflagration relief venting shall be constructed of noncombustible materials.

5.3.4.5 Damage-limiting construction shall be provided in all new construction of the following areas:

(1) Flammable propellant charging rooms
(2) Flammable propellant pump rooms
(3) Areas in which Class IA liquids or unstable liquids are handled

5.3.4.6 Deflagration vents shall relieve to a safe location to avoid injury to personnel and to minimize property damage.

5.3.4.7 Deflagration venting shall be designed and installed in accordance with NFPA 68, *Standard on Explosion Protection by Deflagration Venting*.

5.3.4.8 In existing rooms where deflagration venting cannot be installed, a deflagration suppression system that meets the requirements of NFPA 69, *Standard on Explosion Prevention Systems*, shall be installed.

5.3.4.9 Deflagration vents shall be maintained in accordance with 8.6.3.

5.4 Ventilation.

5.4.1* Mechanical exhaust ventilation shall be provided for flammable concentrate–filling areas and for flammable propellant charging and pump rooms in accordance with 5.4.2 or 5.4.3, as applicable.

5.4.1.1 Ventilation systems shall include exhaust systems and make-up air systems.

5.4.2 Mechanical exhaust ventilation for the flammable propellant charging and pump rooms shall meet the following requirements:

(A) The ventilation shall be nonrecirculating.

(B) Make-up air shall be taken from areas where flammable vapors are not present.

(C) Air inlets and outlets shall be located so that air flows uniformly across the floor of the room. The bottom of the air inlets and outlets shall be no more than 0.15 m (0.5 ft) above the floor.

(D)* The required rate of ventilation shall be determined by the following formula:

$$VR = \frac{(100 - LEL)(V)(R)}{(DL)(LEL)}$$

where:
VR = required ventilation flow rate, m³/hr (ft³/min) (Note: To convert m³/hr to ft³/min, multiply VR by 0.588.)
LEL = lower explosive limit of the specific propellant being used, percent by volume
V = volume of vapor produced per unit volume of liquid propellant, m³/L (ft³/gal)
R = estimated volume of propellant lost during normal filling operations plus 20 percent for occasional system leakage, L/hr (gal/min)
DL = design level, which is the ratio of the desired allowable vapor concentration, in percent by volume, to the lower explosive limit, as defined above (Normally, DL is not more than 0.1.)

Exception: Where provided at all propellant fillers and subject to the approval of the AHJ, local exhaust ventilation shall be permitted to replace up to 75 percent of the volumetric flow rate of the ventilation required by 5.4.2. In no case shall the ventilation rate be less than one air change per minute.

(E) Emergency ventilation shall be activated automatically at not more than 20 percent of the LEL. It shall be designed to provide 150 percent of the air flow rate determined in 5.4.2(D) or two air changes per minute, whichever is greater.

(F)* Exhaust discharge stacks shall be separated horizontally by at least 3 m (10 ft) from make-up air intakes and shall terminate at least 3 m (10 ft) above the roof and at least 1 m (3 ft) above any other building within 7.6 m (25 ft).

(G) Exhaust ventilation air flow shall be monitored so as to enable automatic shutdown of the propellant-filling line in the event of failure of the ventilation system.

(H) All fan blades utilized by the exhaust and make-up air systems shall be nonsparking.

(I) The room shall be maintained at a negative pressure in relation to the ambient air.

5.4.3 Mechanical exhaust ventilation shall be provided for flammable base product–filling areas.

5.4.3.1 For areas that contain production operations likely to emit hazardous concentrations of flammable vapors, general area mechanical ventilation shall be provided at a minimum flow rate of 0.3 m³/min·m² (1 ft³/min·ft²) of floor area.

5.4.3.2 Ventilation shall be arranged to uniformly sweep the entire floor area.

5.4.3.3 When provided at all of the following and subject to the approval of the authority having jurisdiction, local exhaust ventilation shall be permitted to replace up to 75 percent of the volumetric flow rate of the general area ventilation required by 5.4.3:

(1) Base product filler
(2) Button tipper
(3) Valve crimper

5.4.4* Aerosol container test baths shall be enclosed and provided with exhaust ventilation.

5.4.4.1 Exhaust discharge stacks shall meet the requirements of 5.4.2(F).

5.4.5 Local exhaust ventilation shall be provided for reject aerosol container receptacles that are located within buildings.

5.4.6 Fume incinerators shall comply with 5.4.6.1 through 5.4.6.4.

5.4.6.1 Where installed, fume incinerators used to destroy combustible vapors and gases in exhaust ventilation shall be designed and installed in accordance with NFPA 86, *Standard for Ovens and Furnaces*.

5.4.6.2 Where fume incinerators are used, the duct system conveying the vapors shall be monitored by an approved combustible gas detection system.

5.4.6.3 Annunciation of the combustible gas detection system shall occur upon detection of 25 percent of the LEL of the combustible gas.

5.4.6.4 Detection of 50 percent of the LEL of the combustible gas shall activate diverters to direct the vapors to a safe location outdoors.

5.5 Electrical Equipment. Electrical equipment and wiring in flammable propellant charging and pump rooms shall be suitable for Class I, Division 1 or Class I, Zone 1 locations in accordance with Articles 500, 501, 504, and 505 of *NFPA 70, National Electrical Code.*

5.5.1 If the vacuum pumps for propellant charging are installed remotely (i.e., not in the charging room), the area within 1.5 m (5 ft) of the extremities of the pumps shall be classified as a Class I, Division 2 or Class I, Zone 2 location.

5.5.2* Electrical equipment and wiring in areas where flammable liquids are handled shall be suitable for the classification of the area, as defined in Chapters 9 through 16 of NFPA 30, *Flammable and Combustible Liquids Code.*

5.5.3 The area enclosed by the test bath shall be classified as a Class I, Division 1 or Class I, Zone 1 location.

5.5.4 The area within 1.5 m (5 ft) in all directions of the hot tank shall be classified as a Class I, Division 2 or Class I, Zone 2 location.

5.6* Control of Static Electricity. All equipment involved in the manufacture of aerosol products shall be suitably bonded and grounded.

5.7* Combustible Gas Detection Systems.

5.7.1 Flammable propellant charging and pump rooms shall be provided with an approved gas detection system that is equipped with audible or visible alarms.

5.7.2 The gas detection system shall be interlocked in accordance with Section 5.12.

5.7.3 Annunciation of the gas detection system alarm shall be within the charging and pump rooms and in nearby production areas.

5.8 Automatic Sprinkler Protection.

5.8.1* Flammable propellant charging and pump rooms shall be protected by either a wet-pipe or a deluge-type automatic sprinkler system. The system shall be designed to meet the requirements of an extra-hazard, Group II occupancy, as set forth in NFPA 13, *Standard for the Installation of Sprinkler Systems.*

5.8.1.1 Deluge systems shall be activated by an approved detection system.

5.8.2 Production areas that contain base product fillers, button tippers, valve crimpers, test baths, and aerosol can packaging equipment shall be protected by a wet-pipe automatic sprinkler system installed in accordance with NFPA 13, *Standard for the Installation of Sprinkler Systems.* The sprinkler system shall be designed to protect the highest level of storage or production hazard that is present.

5.8.2.1 Storage of up to 1135 kg (2500 lb) net weight of Level 2 or Level 3 aerosol products and aerosol products in plastic containers per production line or rework production line shall be permitted in production areas, such as staging areas (e.g., awaiting transfer to a warehouse), provided they are stacked no more than one palletload high and there is no warehouse storage of aerosol products within 7.6 m (25 ft) of the production line.

5.8.2.1.1 All other storage shall be protected in accordance with Table 6.3.2.7(a) through Table 6.3.2.7(l), as applicable.

5.8.3 Where acceptable to the authority having jurisdiction, an automatic sprinkler system shall be permitted to be equipped for the injection of aqueous film-forming foam (AFFF). Such systems shall be designed and installed in accordance with the following:

(1) NFPA 11, *Standard for Low-, Medium-, and High-Expansion Foam*
(2) NFPA 13, *Standard for the Installation of Sprinkler Systems*
(3) NFPA 16, *Standard for the Installation of Foam-Water Sprinkler and Foam-Water Spray Systems*

5.9 Fixed Extinguishing Systems. Where automatic fire-extinguishing systems are provided to protect production equipment, such as mixers, solvent tanks, or fixed open containers, such systems shall be designed and installed in accordance with the following, as applicable:

(1) NFPA 11, *Standard for Low-, Medium-, and High-Expansion Foam*
(2) NFPA 12, *Standard on Carbon Dioxide Extinguishing Systems*
(3) NFPA 12A, *Standard on Halon 1301 Fire Extinguishing Systems*
(4) NFPA 16, *Standard for the Installation of Foam-Water Sprinkler and Foam-Water Spray Systems*
(5) NFPA 17, *Standard for Dry Chemical Extinguishing Systems*
(6) NFPA 2001, *Standard on Clean Agent Fire Extinguishing Systems*

5.10 Spill Control.

5.10.1* Drainage systems shall be provided to direct leaks and spills to a safe location.

5.10.2 Curbs, scuppers, or special drainage systems shall be permitted to be used to control the spread of fire.

5.10.3 If drainage systems are connected to public sewers or discharge into public waterways, the drainage systems shall be equipped with traps, separators, or other devices that will divert flow to a safe location.

5.11 Deflagration Suppression Systems.

5.11.1 A deflagration suppression system meeting the requirements of NFPA 69, *Standard on Explosion Prevention Systems,* shall be installed in flammable propellant charging rooms and flammable propellant pump rooms.

5.11.2 Where installed, an engineered deflagration suppression system shall meet the requirements of NFPA 69, *Standard on Explosion Prevention Systems,* and shall use approved radiant energy–sensing fire detectors.

5.12 Equipment Interlocks. Equipment shall be interlocked so that the system inputs listed in Table 5.12 result in the associated process/equipment responses given.

5.13 Process Operating Requirements.

5.13.1 Packaging and Conveyor System.

5.13.1.1 Guide rails, starwheels, can screws (worms), and other parts of the conveying system shall be designed to minimize crushing and tipping of containers.

5.13.1.2 Manual or automatic devices shall be installed to stop packaging machinery and conveyors in the event of a jam.

5.13.1.3 Conveyor systems between the propellant charging room and the production area conveyor openings, when provided with covers or weather shields, shall be open at the bottom; or in locations where environmental conditions affect aerosol products or production equipment, a full enclosure shall be permitted when designed to ensure flammable vapors cannot enter the production area from the conveyor enclosure.

Table 5.12 Equipment Interlocks

System Inputs	Propellant Supply Shutdown	Propellant Venting	Aerosol Line Shutdown	Audible and Visual Alarms	Fire Alarms	Standard Ventilation Rate	Emergency Ventilation Rate
Gas detection at 20% LEL	NR	NR	NR	Yes	NR	NA	On
Gas detection at 40% LEL	Yes	NR	Yes	Yes	NR	NA	On
Loss of ventilation	Yes	Yes	Yes	Yes	NR	NA	NA
Emergency stop	Yes	Yes	Yes	Yes	NR	NA	On
Deflagration suppression system disarm or trouble	Yes	Yes	Yes	Yes	NR	On	NA
Halon 1301 deflagration suppression system actuation	Yes	Yes	Yes	Yes	Yes	Off	Off
Water deflagration suppression system actuation	Yes	Yes	Yes	Yes	Yes	NA	On
Loss of power	Yes	Yes	Yes	Yes	NR	NA	NA
Gas detection system fault	Yes	Yes	Yes	Yes	NR	NA	On
Automatic sprinkler actuation	Yes	Yes	Yes	Yes	Yes	NA	NA

NR = Not required. NA = Not applicable.

5.13.2 Crimper Vacuum Pump Discharge Vent.

5.13.2.1 The discharge vent for the crimper vacuum pump shall terminate at a safe location outside, not less than 3.7 m (12 ft) above adjacent ground level.

5.13.2.2 The vent outlet shall be located or arranged so that flammable gas or vapor will not be trapped by eaves or other obstructions and shall be at least 1.5 m (5 ft) from any building openings.

5.13.3 Propellant Charging Equipment.

5.13.3.1 The propellant pump and all equipment subject to pressure from the pump shall be suitable for the working pressure of the system.

5.13.3.1.1* Pump discharge pressures shall not be limited, provided they do not exceed the working pressure of the system.

5.13.3.2 Vacuum pump and propellant pump discharge piping on any equipment that handles flammable gases or liquids shall meet the requirements of 5.13.3.2(A) through 5.13.3.2(D).

(A) The discharge vent shall terminate at a safe location outside and at least 3 m (10 ft) away from any air intake.

(B) The discharge vent shall terminate at least 3 m (10 ft) above the roof and at least 1 m (3 ft) above the highest point of any building within 7.6 m (25 ft).

(C) When venting liquefied flammable gas propellant charging equipment and piping, liquid shall not be discharged directly to the atmosphere. Expansion chamber, knock-out pots, or equivalent devices shall be utilized so that only vapor is released.

(D) Discharge vent manifolds shall service a single propellant charging or pump room. Discharge vents, where installed, shall be designed so as not to inhibit proper operation of safety relief devices.

5.13.3.3 High pressure propellant booster pumps equipped with backpressure regulating valves and return lines shall be provided with an automatic shutdown device in the return line.

5.13.3.3.1* The shutdown device shall be set so that the high pressure pump shuts down if the pressure in the propellant bypass return piping (downstream of the backpressure regulating valve) reaches a minimum gauge pressure of 345 kPa (50 psi) below the set pressure of hydrostatic relief valves installed in the propellant bypass return piping.

5.13.4 Flammable Liquid Propellant Pump.

5.13.4.1 If located inside a building, the propellant pump shall be located either in the propellant charging room or in a separate pump room having suitable ventilation, as described in Section 5.4.

5.13.4.2 If located outside, the propellant charging pump shall be located at least 7.6 m (25 ft) from the following:

(1) Any opening in the adjacent wall of the production facility
(2) Walls or buildings other than the production facility or propellant charging room
(3) Any area subject to vehicular travel
(4) Other sources of ignition

(A) The propellant charging pump shall be placed on a finished noncombustible hard surface.

(B) A clearance of a minimum 3 m (10 ft) shall be required in all directions to vegetation or other combustible materials.

5.13.4.3 Pressure-containing metal parts shall be constructed of the following materials:

(1) Steel
(2) Stainless steel
(3) Ductile (nodular) iron (ASTM A 395 or A 536, grade 60-40-18 or 65-45-12)
(4) Malleable iron (ASTM A 47)
(5) Higher-strength grey iron (ASTM A 48, Class 40B)
(6) Brass
(7) Other materials equivalent to (1) through (6)

5.13.4.4 Pressure-containing parts, plungers, or pistons shall not be constructed of ceramic materials.

5.13.4.5 Bypass regulator bonnet vents, safety relief valves, and hydrostatic relief valves on equipment located within buildings shall be vented to a safe location outside. Discharge vents shall terminate at least 3 m (10 ft) above the roof and at least 1 m (3 ft) above the highest point of any building within 7.6 m (25 ft).

5.13.5 Test Baths.

5.13.5.1 When test baths are heated, they shall be heated with steam or hot water.

5.13.5.2 Open-flame heaters shall not be used with Level 2 or Level 3 aerosol products.

5.13.5.3 Provisions shall be made to prevent overheating and subsequent rupture of containers when containers become lodged or stranded in the bath.

5.13.5.4 Heated test baths shall have an independent over-temperature control to prevent the overheating of the bath water. This control system shall not be the same system that regulates the bath temperature. Actuation of the over-temperature control shall require a manual test.

5.14* Shrink-Wrapping of Aerosol Products.

5.14.1 Where heat shrink-wrapping in tunnel equipment greater than 1.8 m (6 ft) in length of individual packages of 5 or more aerosol cans or palletized aerosol products are performed, the heat shrink-wrap tunnel and equipment shall be provided with the following:

(1) Equipment failure detection and notification
(2) Automatic product evacuation and notification upon loss of power
(3) Automatic fire suppression and notification

5.14.2 Where heat shrink-wrapping in tunnel equipment of 1.8 m (6 ft) or less in length of individual packages of 4 or fewer aerosol cans is performed, an automatic product evacuation system and alarm shall be provided that activates upon loss of power.

5.15 Aerosol Product Laboratories.

5.15.1 Aerosol laboratories shall be considered as Class A laboratory units and, as such, shall comply with NFPA 45, *Standard on Fire Protection for Laboratories Using Chemicals*.

5.15.2 Tests for total discharge, rate of spray, spray pattern, and net weight shall be conducted with proper ventilation.

5.15.3 When the entire contents of an aerosol container must be used to perform a test or the contents of the container must be removed for internal examination of the container, the following precautions shall be taken:

(1) The container shall be placed in a laboratory hood.
(2) The container shall be grounded.
(3) The container shall be pierced with a nonsparking device.
(4) Only one container at a time shall be punctured or sprayed.
(5) When more than one container is to be evacuated at a time, the operation shall be conducted in the propellant charging room, outdoors, or within equipment or facilities specifically designed for this purpose.

5.15.4 Where propellant-filling equipment is similar to that utilized within production operations, the laboratory shall be considered to be a pilot plant and shall meet the construction and ventilation requirements of Chapter 5 of this code.

5.15.4.1 Cold-filling of flammable propellant shall be prohibited for standard or routine evaluations.

5.15.4.2 Cold-filling of small numbers of samples used for special testing shall be permitted where alternate filling methods cannot be used.

5.15.4.3 Manual filling of flammable propellant in an aerosol laboratory shall be conducted inside a well-ventilated laboratory hood.

Chapter 6 Storage in Warehouses and Storage Areas

6.1 Basic Requirements.

6.1.1 The protection criteria in this chapter are for metal containers only. Protection criteria for glass or plastic containers greater than 118 ml (4 fl oz) is beyond the scope of this chapter, with the exception of the maximum allowable quantities (MAQ).

6.1.2 All outer packaging, including cartons, trays, shrouds, or other packaging, of aerosol products shall be identified on at least one side with the classification of the aerosol products in accordance with Section 1.8 and marked as follows:

Level _____ Aerosols

6.1.3* Fire-retardant cartons shall not be considered an acceptable alternative to the protection requirements of Chapter 6.

6.2* Storage of Level 1 Aerosol Products.

6.2.1 Level 1 aerosol products shall be considered equivalent to Class III commodities, as defined in NFPA 13, *Standard for the Installation of Sprinkler Systems*.

6.2.2 In cases where the storage of Level 1 aerosol products is required to be protected, such storage shall be protected in accordance with the requirements for Class III commodities set forth in NFPA 13, *Standard for the Installation of Sprinkler Systems*.

6.3 Storage of Level 2 and Level 3 Aerosol Products.

6.3.1 The storage of Level 2 and Level 3 aerosol products shall be in accordance with Section 6.3.

6.3.1.1 Level 2 aerosol products in containers whose net weight is less than 28 g (1 oz) shall be considered to be equivalent to cartoned unexpanded Group A plastics, as defined in NFPA 13, *Standard for the Installation of Sprinkler Systems*.

6.3.1.1.1 In cases where the storage of Level 2 aerosol products in containers whose net weight is less than 28 g (1 oz) is required to be protected, such storage shall be in accordance with the requirements set forth in NFPA 13, *Standard for the Installation of Sprinkler Systems*, for cartoned unexpanded Group A plastics.

6.3.2 Fire Protection — Basic Requirements.

6.3.2.1 Storage of Level 2 and Level 3 aerosol products shall not be permitted in basement areas of warehouses.

6.3.2.1.1 Storage of Level 2 and Level 3 aerosol products shall be permitted as provided for in 6.3.3.

6.3.2.2* Encapsulated storage of cartoned Level 2 and Level 3 aerosol products shall be protected as uncartoned.

6.3.2.2.1 Stretch-wrapping of cartons of aerosol products shall be permitted.

6.3.2.2.2 Encapsulated storage of uncartoned Level 2 and Level 3 aerosol products on slip sheets or in trays shall be permitted.

6.3.2.3 Level 2 and Level 3 aerosol products whose containers are designed to vent at gauge pressures of less than 1450 kPa (210 psi) shall not be stored.

6.3.2.4 Noncombustible draft curtains shall extend down a minimum of 0.61 m (2 ft) from the ceiling and shall be installed at the interface between ordinary and high-temperature sprinklers.

6.3.2.5 Storage of mixed commodities within or adjacent to aerosol product storage areas shall meet all applicable requirements of Chapter 6.

6.3.2.6 Storage of idle or empty pallets shall meet all applicable requirements of NFPA 13, *Standard for the Installation of Sprinkler Systems*.

6.3.2.7 Where required by Chapter 6, wet-pipe automatic sprinkler protection shall be provided in accordance with Table 6.3.2.7(a) through Table 6.3.2.7(l) and Figure 6.3.2.7(a) through Figure 6.3.2.7(e) as designated in the corresponding table(s).

Table 6.3.2.7(a) Palletized and Solid Pile Storage of Cartoned Level 2 and Level 3 Aerosols (Metric Units)

Aerosol Level	Maximum Ceiling Height (m)	Maximum Storage Height (m)	Sprinkler Type/Nominal Orifice (L/min/bar$^{0.5}$)	Response/Nominal Temperature Rating	Design Density/Area (# sprinklers @ discharge pressure)	Water Supply Duration (hr)	Hose Stream Demand (L/min)
2	7.6	5.5	Large Drop K = 160	SR/Ordinary	15 @ 3.4 bar	2	1900
		6.1	ESFR-pendent K = 200	QR/Ordinary	12 @ 3.4 bar	1	950
			ESFR-pendent K = 240	QR/Ordinary	12 @ 2.4 bar	1	950
			ESFR-pendent K = 320	QR/Ordinary	12 @ 1.7 bar	1	950
			ESFR-pendent K = 360	QR/Ordinary	12 @ 1.7 bar	1	950
	9.1	1.5	Spray K ≥ 115	SR/High	12 mm/min over 232 m²	2	1900
		4.6	ESFR-pendent K = 200	QR/Ordinary	12 @ 3.4 bar	1	950
			ESFR-pendent K = 240	QR/Ordinary	12 @ 2.4 bar	1	950
			ESFR-pendent K = 320	QR/Ordinary	12 @ 1.7 bar	1	950
			ESFR-pendent K = 360	QR/Ordinary	12 @ 1.7 bar	1	950
3	6.1	1.5	Spray K ≥ 115	SR/High	12 mm/min over 232 m²	2	1900
		3.0	Large Drop K = 160	SR/Ordinary	15 @ 5.2 bar	2	1900
	7.6	4.6	ESFR-pendent K = 200	QR/Ordinary	12 @ 3.4 bar	1	950
			ESFR-pendent K = 240	QR/Ordinary	12 @ 2.4 bar	1	950
			ESFR-pendent K = 320	QR/Ordinary	12 @ 1.7 bar	1	950
			ESFR-pendent K = 360	QR/Ordinary	12 @ 1.7 bar	1	950
	9.1	1.5	Spray K ≥ 160	SR/High	25 mm/min over 232 m²	2	1900
		4.6	ESFR-pendent K = 200	QR/Ordinary	12 @ 5.2 bar	1	950
			ESFR-pendent K = 240	QR/Ordinary	12 @ 3.6 bar	1	950
			ESFR-pendent K = 320	QR/Ordinary	12 @ 3.1 bar	1	950
			ESFR-pendent K = 360	QR/Ordinary	12 @ 1.7 bar	1	950

QR: Quick response. SR: Standard response. ESFR: Early suppression fast response.

Table 6.3.2.7(b) Palletized and Solid Pile Storage of Cartoned Level 2 and Level 3 Aerosols (English Units)

Aerosol Level	Maximum Ceiling Height (ft)	Maximum Storage Height (ft)	Sprinkler Type/Nominal Orifice (gpm/psi$^{0.5}$)	Response/Nominal Temperature Rating	Design Density/Area (# sprinklers @ discharge pressure)	Water Supply Duration (hr)	Hose Stream Demand (gpm)
2	25	18	Large Drop K = 11.6	SR/Ordinary	15 @ 50 psi	2	500
		20	ESFR-pendent K = 14.0	QR/Ordinary	12 @ 50 psi	1	250
			ESFR-pendent K = 16.8	QR/Ordinary	12 @ 35 psi	1	250
			ESFR-pendent K = 22.4	QR/Ordinary	12 @ 25 psi	1	250
			ESFR-pendent K = 25.2	QR/Ordinary	12 @ 25 psi	1	250
	30	5	Spray K ≥ 8.0	SR/High	0.30 gpm/ft^2 over 2500 ft^2	2	500
		15	ESFR-pendent K = 14.0	QR/Ordinary	12 @ 50 psi	1	250
			ESFR-pendent K = 16.8	QR/Ordinary	12 @ 35 psi	1	250
			ESFR-pendent K = 22.4	QR/Ordinary	12 @ 25 psi	1	250
			ESFR-pendent K = 25.2	QR/Ordinary	12 @ 25 psi	1	250
3	20	5	Spray K ≥ 8.0	SR/High	0.30 gpm/ft^2 over 2500 ft^2	2	500
		10	Large Drop K = 11.6	SR/Ordinary	15 @ 75 psi	2	500
	25	15	ESFR-pendent K = 14.0	QR/Ordinary	12 @ 50 psi	1	250
			ESFR-pendent K = 16.8	QR/Ordinary	12 @ 35 psi	1	250
			ESFR-pendent K = 22.4	QR/Ordinary	12 @ 25 psi	1	250
			ESFR-pendent K = 25.2	QR/Ordinary	12 @ 25 psi	1	250
	30	5	Spray K ≥ 11.2	SR/High	0.60 gpm/ft^2 over 2500 ft^2	2	500
		15	ESFR-pendent K = 14.0	QR/Ordinary	12 @ 75 psi	1	250
			ESFR-pendent K = 16.8	QR/Ordinary	12 @ 52 psi	1	250
			ESFR-pendent K = 22.4	QR/Ordinary	12 @ 45 psi	1	250
			ESFR-pendent K = 25.2	QR/Ordinary	12 @ 25 psi	1	250

QR: Quick response. SR: Standard response. ESFR: Early suppression fast response.

Table 6.3.2.7(c) Palletized and Solid Pile Storage of Uncartoned Level 2 Aerosols (Metric Units)

Maximum Ceiling Height (m)	Maximum Storage Height (m)	Sprinkler Type/ Nominal Orifice (L/min/bar$^{0.5}$)	Response/ Nominal Temperature Rating	Design Density/Area (# sprinklers @ discharge pressure)	Water Supply Duration (hr)	Hose Stream Demand (L/min)
7.6	4.6	ESFR-pendent K = 200	QR/Ordinary	12 @ 3.4 bar	1	950
		ESFR-pendent K = 240	QR/Ordinary	12 @ 2.4 bar	1	950
		ESFR-pendent K = 320	QR/Ordinary	12 @ 1.7 bar	1	950
		ESFR-pendent K = 360	QR/Ordinary	12 @ 1.7 bar	1	950
9.1	4.6	ESFR-pendent K = 200	QR/Ordinary	12 @ 5.2 bar	1	950
		ESFR-pendent K = 240	QR/Ordinary	12 @ 3.6 bar	1	950
		ESFR-pendent K = 320	QR/Ordinary	12 @ 3.1 bar	1	950
		ESFR-pendent K = 360	QR/Ordinary	12 @ 1.7 bar	1	950

QR: = Quick response. ESFR: Early suppression fast response.

Protection shall be based on the highest level of aerosol product present. No protection criteria have been established for the protection of palletized and solid piled storage of uncartoned Level 3 aerosol products. The tables are as follows:

(1) Table 6.3.2.7(a) Palletized and Solid Pile Storage of Cartoned Level 2 and Level 3 Aerosols (Metric Units)
(2) Table 6.3.2.7(b) Palletized and Solid Pile Storage of Cartoned Level 2 and Level 3 Aerosols (English Units)
(3) Table 6.3.2.7(c) Palletized and Solid Pile Storage of Uncartoned Level 2 Aerosols (Metric Units)
(4) Table 6.3.2.7(d) Palletized and Solid Pile Storage of Uncartoned Level 2 Aerosols (English Units)
(5) Table 6.3.2.7(e) Rack Storage of Cartoned Level 2 Aerosols (Metric Units)
(6) Table 6.3.2.7(f) Rack Storage of Cartoned Level 2 Aerosols (English Units)
(7) Table 6.3.2.7(g) Rack Storage of Cartoned Level 3 Aerosols (Metric Units)
(8) Table 6.3.2.7(h) Rack Storage of Cartoned Level 3 Aerosols (English Units)
(9) Table 6.3.2.7(i) Rack Storage of Uncartoned Level 2 Aerosols (Metric Units)
(10) Table 6.3.2.7(j) Rack Storage of Uncartoned Level 2 Aerosols (English Units)
(11) Table 6.3.2.7(k) Rack Storage of Uncartoned Level 3 Aerosols (Metric Units)
(12) Table 6.3.2.7(l) Rack Storage of Uncartoned Level 3 Aerosols (English Units)

6.3.2.8 Protection criteria that are developed based on full-scale fire tests performed at an approved test facility shall be considered an acceptable alternative to the protection criteria set forth in Table 6.3.2.7(a) through Table 6.3.2.7(l). Such alternative protection criteria shall be subject to the approval of the AHJ.

6.3.2.9* Installation of in-rack sprinklers shall be in accordance with NFPA 13, *Standard for the Installation of Sprinkler Systems*, as modified by Table 6.3.2.7(e) through Table 6.3.2.7(l).

6.3.2.9.1 The in-rack sprinkler water demand shall be based on the simultaneous operation of the most hydraulically remote sprinklers as follows:

(1) Sprinkler design parameters shall be in accordance with the protection tables.
(2) In-rack design flows indicated in Table 6.3.2.7(e) through Table 6.3.2.7(l) shall be provided, but in no case shall the end-sprinkler discharge be less than 1 bar (15 psi).
(3) Eight (8) sprinklers where only one level of in-rack sprinklers is provided.

Table 6.3.2.7(d) Palletized and Solid Pile Storage of Uncartoned Level 2 Aerosols (English Units)

Maximum Ceiling Height (ft)	Maximum Storage Height (ft)	Sprinkler Type/Nominal Orifice (gpm/psi$^{0.5}$)	Response/ Nominal Temperature Rating	Design Density/Area (# sprinklers @ discharge pressure)	Water Supply Duration (hr)	Hose Stream Demand (gpm)
25	15	ESFR-pendent K = 14.0	QR/Ordinary	12 @ 50 psi	1	250
		ESFR-pendent K = 16.8	QR/Ordinary	12 @ 35 psi	1	250
		ESFR-pendent K = 22.4	QR/Ordinary	12 @ 25 psi	1	250
		ESFR-pendent K = 25.2	QR/Ordinary	12 @ 25 psi	1	250
30	15	ESFR-pendent K = 14.0	QR/Ordinary	12 @ 75 psi	1	250
		ESFR-pendent K = 16.8	QR/Ordinary	12 @ 52 psi	1	250
		ESFR-pendent K = 22.4	QR/Ordinary	12 @ 45 psi	1	250
		ESFR-pendent K = 25.2	QR/Ordinary	12 @ 25 psi	1	250

QR: Quick response. ESFR: Early suppression fast response.

(4) Twelve (12) sprinklers [six (6) sprinklers on two levels] where only two levels of in-rack sprinklers are provided.
(5) Eighteen (18) sprinklers [six (6) sprinklers on the top three levels] where more than 2 levels of in-rack sprinklers are provided.

6.3.2.10 Installations of hose connections shall meet the requirements of NFPA 13, *Standard for the Installation of Sprinkler Systems.*

6.3.2.10.1 Subject to the approval of the AHJ, hose stations shall not be required to be installed in storage areas.

6.3.2.11 Storage height and building heights shall comply with Table 6.3.2.7(a) through Table 6.3.2.7(l).

6.3.2.12 Solid shelving shall comply with 6.3.2.12.1 through 6.3.2.12.3.

6.3.2.12.1 Solid shelving that is installed in racks that contain Level 2 and Level 3 aerosol products shall be protected in accordance with Table 6.3.2.7(e) through Table 6.3.2.7(l), whichever is applicable.

6.3.2.12.2 In addition to the in-rack sprinklers shown in Figure 6.3.2.7(a) through Figure 6.3.2.7(e), whichever is applicable, a face sprinkler shall be provided directly below the solid shelf or the elevation of the solid shelf if the face sprinkler is located in a transverse flue.

6.3.2.12.3 The face sprinklers below the shelving required by 6.3.2.12.2 shall be not greater than 2.4 m (8 ft) apart as far as the solid shelving level extends.

6.3.2.13 Where spray sprinklers are utilized for ceiling protection, sprinkler spacing shall not exceed 9.3 m^2 (100 ft^2) unless otherwise permitted by 6.3.2.14.

6.3.2.14 Ordinary or intermediate temperature rated K = 25.2 extended-coverage spray sprinklers shall be permitted to be used for all density spray sprinkler design criteria in Table 6.3.2.7(a) through Table 6.3.2.7(l) when installed in accordance with their listing.

6.3.2.15 The ceiling heights in Table 6.3.2.7(e) through Table 6.3.2.7(l) shall be permitted to be increased by a maximum of 10 percent if an equivalent percent increase in ceiling sprinkler design density is provided. This shall only apply to spray sprinkler protection criteria.

Table 6.3.2.7(e) Rack Storage of Cartoned Level 2 Aerosols (Metric Units)

Maximum Roof Height (m)	Maximum Storage Height (m)	Ceiling Sprinkler Protection Criteria - Sprinkler Type/Nominal Orifice (L/min/bar$^{0.5}$)	Response/Nominal Temperature Rating	Design Density/Area (# sprinklers @ discharge pressure)	In-Rack Sprinkler Protection Criteria - Layout	Sprinkler Type/Nominal Orifice (L/min/bar$^{0.5}$)	Response/Nominal Temperature Rating	Discharge Flow (L/min)	Hose Stream Demand (L/min)	Water Supply Duration (hr)
7.6	6.1	ESFR-pendent K = 200	QR/Ordinary	12 @ 3.4 bar	NA	NA	NA	NA	950	1
		ESFR-pendent K = 240	QR/Ordinary	12 @ 2.4 bar	NA	NA	NA	NA	950	1
		ESFR-pendent K = 320	QR/Ordinary	12 @ 1.7 bar	NA	NA	NA	NA	950	1
		ESFR-pendent K = 360	QR/Ordinary	12 @ 1.7 bar	NA	NA	NA	NA	950	1
9.1	4.6	ESFR-pendent K = 200	QR/Ordinary	12 @ 3.4 bar	NA	NA	NA	NA	950	1
		ESFR-pendent K = 240	QR/Ordinary	12 @ 2.4 bar	NA	NA	NA	NA	950	1
		ESFR-pendent K = 320	QR/Ordinary	12 @ 1.7 bar	NA	NA	NA	NA	950	1
		ESFR-pendent K = 360	QR/Ordinary	12 @ 1.7 bar	NA	NA	NA	NA	950	1
	6.1	Spray K ≥ 115	SR/High	12 mm/min over 232 m²	Figure 6.3.2.7(a)	Spray K-80 or K-115	QR/Ordinary	114	1900	2
	7.6	ESFR-pendent K = 200	QR/Ordinary	12 @ 3.4 bar	Figure 6.3.2.7(a)	Spray K-80 or K-115	QR/Ordinary	114	950	1
		ESFR-pendent K = 240	QR/Ordinary	12 @ 2.4 bar	Figure 6.3.2.7(a)	Spray K-80 or K-115	QR/Ordinary	114	950	1
		ESFR-pendent K = 320	QR/Ordinary	12 @ 1.7 bar	Figure 6.3.2.7(a)	Spray K-80 or K-115	QR/Ordinary	114	950	1
		ESFR-pendent K = 360	QR/Ordinary	12 @ 1.7 bar	Figure 6.3.2.7(a)	Spray K-80 or K-115	QR/Ordinary	114	950	1
		Spray K ≥ 160	SR/High	16 mm/min over 232 m²	Figure 6.3.2.7(a)	Spray K-80 or K-115	SR or QR/Ordinary	114	1900	2
Unlimited	Unlimited	See Protection for Level 3 Aerosols with Unlimited Building and Storage Heights								

QR: Quick response. SR: Standard response. ESFR: Early suppression fast response. NA: Not applicable.
Note: See 6.3.2.9.1 for in-rack sprinkler design.

6.3.2.16 Protection systems that are designed and developed based on full-scale fire tests performed at an approved test facility or on other engineered protection schemes shall be considered an acceptable alternative to the protection criteria set forth in Section 6.3. Such alternative protection systems shall be approved by the AHJ.

6.3.2.17 Rack storage shall be arranged so that a minimum aisle width of 2.4 m (8 ft) is maintained between rows of racks and between racks and adjacent solid pile or palletized storage.

6.3.2.18 Where protection is provided by ESFR sprinklers, aisle width shall be not less than 1.2 m (4 ft).

6.3.2.19 Solid pile and palletized storage shall be arranged so that no storage is more than 7.6 m (25 ft) from an aisle. Aisles shall be not less than 1.2 m (4 ft) wide.

6.3.3 Limited-Quantity Storage in Occupancies Other Than Warehouses.

6.3.3.1 Storage of Level 2 and Level 3 aerosol products and aerosol products in plastic containers in a single fire area in occupancies other than warehouses or mercantile occupancies, such as assembly, business, educational, industrial, and institutional occupancies, shall be permitted up to one of the following quantities:

(1) A maximum of 454 kg (1000 lb) net weight of Level 2 aerosol products
(2) A maximum of 227 kg (500 lb) net weight of Level 3 aerosol products
(3) A maximum of 227 kg (500 lb) net weight of aerosol products in plastic containers

Table 6.3.2.7(f) Rack Storage of Cartoned Level 2 Aerosols (English Units)

| Maximum Roof Height (ft) | Maximum Storage Height (ft) | Ceiling Sprinkler Protection Criteria ||| In-Rack Sprinkler Protection Criteria |||| Hose Stream Demand (gpm) | Water Supply Duration (hr) |
		Sprinkler Type/Nominal Orifice (gpm/psi$^{0.5}$)	Response/ Nominal Temperature Rating	Design Density/Area (# sprinklers @ discharge pressure)	Layout	Sprinkler Type/Nominal Orifice (gpm/psi$^{0.5}$)	Response/ Nominal Temperature Rating	Discharge Flow (gpm)		
25	20	ESFR-pendent K = 14.0	QR/Ordinary	12 @ 50 psi	NA	NA	NA	NA	250	1
		ESFR-pendent K = 16.8	QR/Ordinary	12 @ 35 psi	NA	NA	NA	NA	250	1
		ESFR-pendent K = 22.4	QR/Ordinary	12 @ 25 psi	NA	NA	NA	NA	250	1
		ESFR-pendent K = 25.2	QR/Ordinary	12 @ 25 psi	NA	NA	NA	NA	250	1
30	15	ESFR-pendent K = 14.0	QR/Ordinary	12 @ 50 psi	NA	NA	NA	NA	250	1
		ESFR-pendent K = 16.8	QR/Ordinary	12 @ 35 psi	NA	NA	NA	NA	250	1
		ESFR-pendent K = 22.4	QR/Ordinary	12 @ 25 psi	NA	NA	NA	NA	250	1
		ESFR-pendent K = 25.2	QR/Ordinary	12 @ 25 psi	NA	NA	NA	NA	250	1
	20	Spray K ≥ 8.0	SR/High	0.3 gpm/ft^2 over 2500 ft^2	Figure 6.3.2.7(a)	Spray K- 5.6 or K-8	QR / Ordinary	30	500	2
	25	ESFR-pendent K = 14.0	QR/Ordinary	12 @ 50 psi	Figure 6.3.2.7(a)	Spray K- 5.6 or K-8	QR / Ordinary	30	250	1
		ESFR-pendent K = 16.8	QR/Ordinary	12 @ 35 psi	Figure 6.3.2.7(a)	Spray K- 5.6 or K-8	QR / Ordinary	30	250	1
		ESFR-pendent K = 22.4	QR/Ordinary	12 @ 25 psi	Figure 6.3.2.7(a)	Spray K- 5.6 or K-8	QR / Ordinary	30	250	1
		ESFR-pendent K = 25.2	QR/Ordinary	12 @ 25 psi	Figure 6.3.2.7(a)	Spray K- 5.6 or K-8	QR / Ordinary	30	250	1
		Spray K ≥ 11.2	SR/High	0.4 gpm/ft^2 over 2500 ft^2	Figure 6.3.2.7(a)	Spray K- 5.6 or K-8	SR or QR / Ordinary	30	500	2
Unlimited	Unlimited	See Protection for Level 3 Aerosols with Unlimited Building and Storage Heights								

QR: Quick response. SR: Standard response. ESFR: Early suppression fast response. NA: Not applicable.
Note: See 6.3.2.9.1 for in-rack sprinkler design.

6.3.3.2 In no case shall the combined net weight of Level 2 and Level 3 aerosol products and aerosol products in plastic containers exceed 454 kg (1000 lb).

6.3.3.3 These quantities shall be permitted to be doubled if the quantities in excess of those stated in 6.3.3.1 are stored in storage cabinets that meet the requirements of Section 9.5 of NFPA 30, *Flammable and Combustible Liquids Code*.

6.3.3.4 Where Level 2 and Level 3 aerosol products are stored in quantities greater than those allowed by 6.3.3.1 and 6.3.3.2, such quantities shall be stored in a separate inside storage area meeting the requirements of 6.3.7.

6.3.4 Limited-Quantity Storage in General-Purpose Warehouses.

6.3.4.1 Subject to the approval of the AHJ, solid pile, palletized, or rack storage of Level 2 and Level 3 aerosol products and aerosol products in plastic containers shall be permitted in a general-purpose warehouse that is either unsprinklered or not protected in accordance with this code, up to one of the following quantities:

(1) A maximum of 1135 kg (2500 lb) net weight of Level 2 aerosol products
(2) A maximum of 454 kg (1000 lb) net weight of Level 3 aerosol products
(3) A maximum of 454 kg (1000 lb) net weight of aerosol products in plastic containers

6.3.4.2 In no case shall the combined net weight of Level 2 and Level 3 aerosol products and aerosol products in plastic containers exceed 1135 kg (2500 lb).

Table 6.3.2.7(g) Rack Storage of Cartoned Level 3 Aerosols (Metric Units)

| Maximum Roof Height (m) | Maximum Storage Height (m) | Ceiling Sprinkler Protection Criteria ||| In-Rack Sprinkler Protection Criteria |||| Hose Stream Demand (L/min) | Water Supply Duration (hr) |
		Sprinkler Type/ Nominal Orifice (L/min/bar$^{0.5}$)	Response/ Nominal Temperature Rating	Design Density/Area (# sprinklers @ discharge pressure)	Layout	Sprinkler Type/Nominal Orifice (L/min/bar$^{0.5}$)	Response/ Nominal Temperature Rating	Discharge Flow (L/min)		
7.6	4.6	ESFR-pendent K = 200	QR/Ordinary	12 @ 3.4 bar	NA	NA	NA	NA	950	1
		ESFR-pendent K = 240	QR/Ordinary	12 @ 2.4 bar	NA	NA	NA	NA	950	1
		ESFR-pendent K = 320	QR/Ordinary	12 @ 1.7 bar	NA	NA	NA	NA	950	1
		ESFR-pendent K = 360	QR/Ordinary	12 @ 1.7 bar	NA	NA	NA	NA	950	1
9.1	4.6	ESFR-pendent K = 200	QR/Ordinary	12 @ 5.2 bar	NA	NA	NA	NA	950	1
		ESFR-pendent K = 240	QR/Ordinary	12 @ 3.6 bar	NA	NA	NA	NA	950	1
		ESFR-pendent K = 320	QR/Ordinary	12 @ 3.1 bar	NA	NA	NA	NA	950	1
		ESFR-pendent K = 360	QR/Ordinary	12 @ 1.7 bar	NA	NA	NA	NA	950	1
	7.6	ESFR-pendent K = 200	QR/Ordinary	12 @ 5.2 bar	Figure 6.3.2.7(a) or (b)	Spray K-80 or K-115	QR / Ordinary	114	950	1
		ESFR-pendent K = 240	QR/Ordinary	12 @ 3.6 bar	Figure 6.3.2.7(a) or (b)	Spray K-80 or K-115	QR / Ordinary	114	950	1
		ESFR-pendent K = 320	QR/Ordinary	12 @ 3.1 bar	Figure 6.3.2.7(a) or (b)	Spray K-80 or K-115	QR / Ordinary	114	950	1
		ESFR-pendent K = 360	QR/Ordinary	12 @ 1.7 bar	Figure 6.3.2.7(a) or (b)	Spray K-80 or K-115	QR / Ordinary	114	950	1
		Spray K ≥ 160	SR/High	25 mm/min over 232 m^2	Figure 6.3.2.7(a)	Spray K-80 or K-115	SR or QR / Ordinary	114	1900	2
		Spray K ≥ 115	SR/High	12 mm/min over 232 m^2	Figure 6.3.2.7(b)	Spray K-80 or K-115	SR or QR / Ordinary	114	1900	2
Unlimited	For Clearance ≤ 1.5 m	Spray K ≥ 160	SR/High	25 mm/min over 140 m^2	Figure 6.3.2.7(b)	Spray K-80 or K-115	SR or QR / Ordinary	114	1900	2
	For Clearance > 1.5 m & < 4.6 m	Spray K ≥ 160	SR/High	25 mm/min over 140 m^2 to 232 m^2 Interpolate for clearances between 1.5 m and 4.6 m.	Figure 6.3.2.7(b)	Spray K-80 or K-115	SR or QR / Ordinary	114	1900	2
	For Clearance > 4.6 m	Spray K ≥ 115	SR/High	12 mm/min over 232 m^2	Figure 6.3.2.7(c)	Spray K-80 or K-115	SR or QR / Ordinary	114	1900	2

QR: Quick response. SR: Standard response. ESFR: Early suppression fast response. NA: Not applicable.
Note: See 6.3.2.9.1 for in-rack sprinkler design.

Table 6.3.2.7(h) Rack Storage of Cartoned Level 3 Aerosols (English Units)

| Maximum Roof Height (ft) | Maximum Storage Height (ft) | Ceiling Sprinkler Protection Criteria ||| In-Rack Sprinkler Protection Criteria |||| Hose Stream Demand (gpm) | Water Supply Duration (hr) |
		Sprinkler Type/ Nominal Orifice (gpm/psi$^{0.5}$)	Response/ Nominal Temperature Rating	Design Density/Area (# sprinklers @ discharge pressure)	Layout	Sprinkler Type/Nominal Orifice (gpm/psi$^{0.5}$)	Response/ Nominal Temperature Rating	Discharge Flow (gpm)		
25	15	ESFR-pendent K = 14.0	QR/Ordinary	12 @ 50 psi	NA	NA	NA	NA	250	1
		ESFR-pendent K = 16.8	QR/Ordinary	12 @ 35 psi	NA	NA	NA	NA	250	1
		ESFR-pendent K = 22.4	QR/Ordinary	12 @ 25 psi	NA	NA	NA	NA	250	1
		ESFR-pendent K = 25.2	QR/Ordinary	12 @ 25 psi	NA	NA	NA	NA	250	1
30	15	ESFR-pendent K = 14.0	QR/Ordinary	12 @ 75 psi	NA	NA	NA	NA	250	1
		ESFR-pendent K = 16.8	QR/Ordinary	12 @ 52 psi	NA	NA	NA	NA	250	1
		ESFR-pendent K = 22.4	QR/Ordinary	12 @ 45 psi	NA	NA	NA	NA	250	1
		ESFR-pendent K = 25.2	QR/Ordinary	12 @ 25 psi	NA	NA	NA	NA	250	1
	25	ESFR-pendent K = 14.0	QR/Ordinary	12 @ 75 psi	Figure 6.3.2.7(a) or (b)	Spray K-5.6 or K-8	QR/Ordinary	30	250	1
		ESFR-pendent K = 16.8	QR/Ordinary	12 @ 52 psi	Figure 6.3.2.7(a) or (b)	Spray K-5.6 or K-8	QR/Ordinary	30	250	1
		ESFR-pendent K = 22.4	QR/Ordinary	12 @ 45 psi	Figure 6.3.2.7(a) or (b)	Spray K-5.6 or K-8	QR/Ordinary	30	250	1
		ESFR-pendent K = 25.2	QR/Ordinary	12 @ 25 psi	Figure 6.3.2.7(a) or (b)	Spray K-5.6 or K-8	QR/Ordinary	30	250	1
		Spray K ≥ 11.2	SR/High	0.60 gpm/ft^2 over 2500 ft^2	Figure 6.3.2.7(a)	Spray K-5.6 or K-8	SR or QR/Ordinary	30	500	2
		Spray K ≥ 8.0	SR/High	0.3 gpm/ft^2 over 2500 ft^2	Figure 6.3.2.7(b)	Spray K-5.6 or K-8	SR or QR/Ordinary	30	500	2
Unlimited	For Clearance ≤ 5 ft	Spray K ≥ 11.2	SR/High	0.6 gpm/ft^2 over 1500 ft^2	Figure 6.3.2.7(b)	Spray K-5.6 or K-8	SR or QR/Ordinary	30	500	2
	For Clearance > 5 ft & < 15 ft	Spray K ≥ 11.2	SR/High	0.60 gpm/ft^2 over 1500 ft^2 to 2500 ft^2; interpolate for clearances between 5 ft and 15 ft.	Figure 6.3.2.7(b)	Spray K-5.6 or K-8	SR or QR/Ordinary	30	500	2
	For Clearance > 15 ft	Spray K ≥ 8.0	SR/High	0.30 gpm/ft^2 over 2500 ft^2	Figure 6.3.2.7(c)	Spray K-5.6 or K-8	SR or QR/Ordinary	30	500	2

QR: Quick response. SR: Standard response. ESFR: Early suppression fast response. NA: Not applicable.
Note: See 6.3.2.9.1 for in-rack sprinkler design.

Table 6.3.2.7(i) Rack Storage of Uncartoned Level 2 Aerosols (Metric Units)

Maximum Roof Height (m)	Maximum Storage Height (m)	Sprinkler Type/ Nominal Orifice (L/min/bar$^{0.5}$)	Response/ Nominal Temperature Rating	Design Density/Area (# sprinklers @ discharge pressure)	Layout	Sprinkler Type/Nominal Orifice (L/min/bar$^{0.5}$)	Response/ Nominal Temperature Rating	Discharge Flow (L/min)	Hose Stream Demand (L/min)	Water Supply Duration (hr)
9.1	4.6	ESFR-pendent K = 200	QR/Ordinary	12 @ 5.2 bar	NA	NA	NA	NA	950	1
		ESFR-pendent K = 240	QR/Ordinary	12 @ 3.6 bar	NA	NA	NA	NA	950	1
		ESFR-pendent K = 320	QR/Ordinary	12 @ 3.1 bar	NA	NA	NA	NA	950	1
		ESFR-pendent K = 360	QR/Ordinary	12 @ 1.7 bar	NA	NA	NA	NA	950	1
	6.1	ESFR-pendent K = 200	QR/Ordinary	12 @ 3.4 bar	Figure 6.3.2.7(d)	Spray K-115 or K-160	QR/Ordinary	170	950	1
		ESFR-pendent K = 240	QR/Ordinary	12 @ 2.4 bar	Figure 6.3.2.7(d)	Spray K-115 or K-160	QR/Ordinary	170	950	1
		ESFR-pendent K = 320	QR/Ordinary	12 @ 1.7 bar	Figure 6.3.2.7(d)	Spray K-115 or K-160	QR/Ordinary	170	950	1
		ESFR-pendent K = 360	QR/Ordinary	12 @ 1.7 bar	Figure 6.3.2.7(d)	Spray K-115 or K-160	QR/Ordinary	170	950	1
		Spray K ≥ 160	SR/High	25 mm/min over 186 m²	Figure 6.3.2.7(d)	Spray K-115 or K-160	QR/Ordinary	170	1900	2
		Spray K ≥ 115	SR/High	12 mm/min over 232 m²	Figure 6.3.2.7(e)	Spray K-115 or K-160	QR/Ordinary	170	1900	2
	7.6	ESFR-pendent K = 200	QR/Ordinary	12 @ 3.4 bar	Figure 6.3.2.7(e)	Spray K-115 or K-160	QR/Ordinary	170	950	1
		ESFR-pendent K = 240	QR/Ordinary	12 @ 2.4 bar	Figure 6.3.2.7(e)	Spray K-115 or K-160	QR/Ordinary	170	950	1
		ESFR-pendent K = 320	QR/Ordinary	12 @ 1.7 bar	Figure 6.3.2.7(e)	Spray K-115 or K-160	QR/Ordinary	170	950	1
		ESFR-pendent K = 360	QR/Ordinary	12 @ 1.7 bar	Figure 6.3.2.7(e)	Spray K-115 or K-160	QR/Ordinary	170	950	1
		Spray K ≥ 115	SR/High	12 mm/min over 232 m²	Figure 6.3.2.7(e)	Spray K-115 or K-160	QR/Ordinary	170	1900	2

QR: Quick response. SR: Standard response. ESFR: Early suppression fast response. NA: Not applicable.
Note: See 6.3.2.9.1 for in-rack sprinkler design.

6.3.4.3 Subject to the approval of the AHJ, solid pile or palletized storage of Level 2 and Level 3 aerosol products shall be permitted in a general-purpose warehouse that is protected throughout by an automatic sprinkler system up to a maximum total quantity of 5,450 kg (12,000 lb) combined net weight of Level 2 and Level 3 aerosol products, subject to the following:

(1) The sprinkler system over the aerosol storage area and for a distance of 6 m (20 ft) beyond shall be designed in accordance with Table 6.3.2.7(a) through Table 6.3.2.7(d).
(2) Storage of flammable and combustible liquids shall be separated from the aerosol products storage area by at least 8 m (25 ft).

6.3.4.4 Subject to the approval of the AHJ, rack storage of Level 2 and Level 3 aerosol products shall be permitted in a general-purpose warehouse that is protected throughout by an automatic sprinkler system up to a maximum total quantity of 10,900 kg (24,000 lb) combined net weight of Level 2 and Level 3 aerosol products, subject to the following:

(1) The sprinkler system in the Level 2 and Level 3 aerosol products storage area shall be designed in accordance with Table 6.3.2.7(e) through Table 6.3.2.7(l). The ceiling sprinkler system design shall extend for 6 m (20 ft) beyond the aerosol products storage area.
(2) Storage of aerosol products shall be separated from storage of flammable and combustible liquids by at least 8 m (25 ft).

Table 6.3.2.7(j) Rack Storage of Uncartoned Level 2 Aerosols (English Units)

| Maximum Roof Height (ft) | Maximum Storage Height (ft) | Ceiling Sprinkler Protection Criteria ||| In-Rack Sprinkler Protection Criteria |||| Hose Stream Demand (gpm) | Water Supply Duration (hr) |
		Sprinkler Type/Nominal Orifice (gpm/psi$^{0.5}$)	Response/ Nominal Temperature Rating	Design Density/Area (# sprinklers @ discharge pressure)	Layout	Sprinkler Type/Nominal Orifice (gpm/psi$^{0.5}$)	Response/ Nominal Temperature Rating	Discharge Flow (gpm)		
30	15	ESFR-pendent K = 14.0	QR/Ordinary	12 @ 75 psi	NA	NA	NA	NA	250	1
		ESFR-pendent K = 16.8	QR/Ordinary	12 @ 52 psi	NA	NA	NA	NA	250	1
		ESFR-pendent K = 22.4	QR/Ordinary	12 @ 45 psi	NA	NA	NA	NA	250	1
		ESFR-pendent K = 25.2	QR/Ordinary	12 @ 25 psi	NA	NA	NA	NA	250	1
	20	ESFR-pendent K = 14.0	QR/Ordinary	12 @ 50 psi	Figure 6.3.2.7(d)	Spray K-8 or K-11.2	QR/Ordinary	45	250	1
		ESFR-pendent K = 16.8	QR/Ordinary	12 @ 35 psi	Figure 6.3.2.7(d)	Spray K-8 or K-11.2	QR/Ordinary	45	250	1
		ESFR-pendent K = 22.4	QR/Ordinary	12 @ 25 psi	Figure 6.3.2.7(d)	Spray K-8 or K-11.2	QR/Ordinary	45	250	1
		ESFR-pendent K = 25.2	QR/Ordinary	12 @ 25 psi	Figure 6.3.2.7(d)	Spray K-8 or K-11.2	QR/Ordinary	45	250	1
		Spray K ≥ 11.2	SR/High	0.6 gpm/ft^2 over 2000 ft^2	Figure 6.3.2.7(d)	Spray K-8 or K-11.2	QR/Ordinary	45	500	2
		Spray K ≥ 8.0	SR/High	0.3 gpm/ft^2 over 2500 ft^2	Figure 6.3.2.7(e)	Spray K-8 or K-11.2	QR/Ordinary	45	500	2
	25	ESFR-pendent K = 14.0	QR/Ordinary	12 @ 50 psi	Figure 6.3.2.7(e)	Spray K-8 or K-11.2	QR/Ordinary	45	250	1
		ESFR-pendent K = 16.8	QR/Ordinary	12 @ 35 psi	Figure 6.3.2.7(e)	Spray K-8 or K-11.2	QR/Ordinary	45	250	1
		ESFR-pendent K = 22.4	QR/Ordinary	12 @ 25 psi	Figure 6.3.2.7(e)	Spray K-8 or K-11.2	QR/Ordinary	45	250	1
		ESFR-pendent K = 25.2	QR/Ordinary	12 @ 25 psi	Figure 6.3.2.7(e)	Spray K-8 or K-11.2	QR/Ordinary	45	250	1
		Spray K ≥ 8.0	SR/High	0.3 gpm/ft^2 over 2500 ft^2	Figure 6.3.2.7(e)	Spray K-8 or K-11.2	QR/Ordinary	45	500	2

QR: = Quick response. SR: Standard response. ESFR: Early suppression fast response. NA: Not applicable.
Note: See 6.3.2.9.1 for in-rack sprinkler design.

6.3.5 Segregated Aerosol Product Storage Areas in General-Purpose Warehouses.

6.3.5.1 Segregated storage of Level 2 and Level 3 aerosol products in a general-purpose warehouse shall only be in a warehouse that is protected throughout by an automatic sprinkler system that is designed in accordance with NFPA 13, *Standard for the Installation of Sprinkler Systems*.

6.3.5.2 Solid pile, palletized, or rack storage of Level 2 and Level 3 aerosol products in excess of the maximum quantities given in 6.3.4.1 through 6.3.4.3 shall be protected in accordance with the requirements in 6.3.5.3 through 6.3.5.7.

6.3.5.3 Storage of Level 2 and Level 3 aerosol products shall be in a segregated area separated from the rest of the warehouse by interior walls, chain-link fencing, or a separation area, in accordance with the requirements of 6.3.5.3.1 through 6.3.5.3.3.

6.3.5.3.1 Interior walls shall have a fire resistance rating of 1 or 2 hours and shall be continuous from floor to the underside of the roof deck or ceiling.

6.3.5.3.1.1 Openings in these walls shall be protected with self-closing or automatic-closing listed fire door assemblies

Table 6.3.2.7(k) Rack Storage of Uncartoned Level 3 Aerosols (Metric Units)

Maximum Roof Height (m)	Maximum Storage Height (m)	Ceiling Sprinkler Protection Criteria — Sprinkler Type/Nominal Orifice (L/min/bar$^{0.5}$)	Response/Nominal Temperature Rating	Design Density/Area (# sprinklers @ discharge pressure)	Layout	In-Rack Sprinkler Protection Criteria — Sprinkler Type/Nominal Orifice (L/min/bar$^{0.5}$)	Response/Nominal Temperature Rating	Discharge Flow (L/min)	Hose Stream Demand (L/min)	Water Supply Duration (hr)
9.1	6.1	ESFR-pendent K = 200	QR/Ordinary	12 @ 5.2 bar	Figure 6.3.2.7(d)	Spray K-115 or K-160	QR/Ordinary	170	950	1
		ESFR-pendent K = 240	QR/Ordinary	12 @ 3.6 bar	Figure 6.3.2.7(d)	Spray K-115 or K-160	QR/Ordinary	170	950	1
		ESFR-pendent K = 320	QR/Ordinary	12 @ 3.1 bar	Figure 6.3.2.7(d)	Spray K-115 or K-160	QR/Ordinary	170	950	1
		ESFR-pendent K = 360	QR/Ordinary	12 @ 1.7 bar	Figure 6.3.2.7(d)	Spray K-115 or K-160	QR/Ordinary	170	950	1
		Spray K ≥ 160	SR/High	25 mm/min over 186 m²	Figure 6.3.2.7(d)	Spray K-115 or K-160	QR/Ordinary	170	1900	2
		Spray K ≥ 115	SR/High	12 mm/min over 232 m²	Figure 6.3.2.7(e)	Spray K-115 or K-160	QR/Ordinary	170	1900	2
	7.6	ESFR-pendent K = 200	QR/Ordinary	12 @ 5.2 bar	Figure 6.3.2.7(e)	Spray K-115 or K-160	QR/Ordinary	170	950	1
		ESFR-pendent K = 240	QR/Ordinary	12 @ 3.6 bar	Figure 6.3.2.7(e)	Spray K-115 or K-160	QR/Ordinary	170	950	1
		ESFR-pendent K = 320	QR/Ordinary	12 @ 3.1 bar	Figure 6.3.2.7(e)	Spray K-115 or K-160	QR/Ordinary	170	950	1
		ESFR-pendent K = 360	QR/Ordinary	12 @ 1.7 bar	Figure 6.3.2.7(e)	Spray K-115 or K-160	QR/Ordinary	170	950	1
		Spray K ≥ 115	SR/High	12 mm/min over 232 m²	Figure 6.3.2.7(e)	Spray K-115 or K-160	QR/Ordinary	170	1900	2

QR: Quick response. SR: Standard response. ESFR: Early suppression fast response.
Note: See 6.3.2.9.1 for in-rack sprinkler design.

with fire protection ratings corresponding to the fire resistance rating of the wall as specified in Table 6.3.5.3.1.1.

(A) For interior walls having a fire resistance rating of 2 hours, the total floor area of the segregated Level 2 and Level 3 aerosol storage area(s) shall not exceed 25 percent of the total floor area of the warehouse, up to a maximum of 3,660 m² (40,000 ft²).

(B) For interior walls having a fire resistance rating of 1 hour, the total floor area of the segregated Level 2 and Level 3 aerosol storage area(s) shall not exceed 20 percent of the total floor area of the warehouse, up to a maximum of 2,745 m² (30,000 ft²).

6.3.5.3.2 Chain-link fencing shall extend from the floor to the underside of the roof deck or ceiling and shall meet the following requirements:

(1) The total floor area of the segregated Level 2 and Level 3 aerosol storage area(s) shall not exceed 20 percent of the total area of the warehouse, up to a maximum of 1,830 m² (20,000 ft²).

(2) Fencing shall not be lighter than 2.9 mm (9 gauge) steel wire woven into a maximum 50 mm (2 in.) diamond mesh.
(3) Storage of commodities whose hazard exceeds that of a Class III commodity, as defined by NFPA 13, *Standard for the Installation of Sprinkler Systems*, shall be kept outside of the segregated area and at least 2.4 m (8 ft) from the fence, except as allowed by 6.3.5.7.
(4) The area of the design for the required ceiling sprinkler system shall extend 6 m (20 ft) beyond the segregated area.
(5) A minimum of two personnel exits shall be provided.
(6) All openings in the fencing shall be provided with self-closing or automatic-closing gates or shall be protected with a labyrinth arrangement.
(7) Where automatic-closing gates are used, manual closure actuating devices shall be provided adjacent to the opening to allow for manual closure of the gates.

6.3.5.3.3 Subject to the approval of the AHJ, a separation area shall extend outward from the periphery of the segregated

Table 6.3.2.7(l) Rack Storage of Uncartoned Level 3 Aerosols (English Units)

Maximum Roof Height (ft)	Maximum Storage Height (ft)	Ceiling Sprinkler Protection Criteria — Sprinkler Type/Nominal Orifice (gpm/psi$^{0.5}$)	Response/Nominal Temperature Rating	Design Density/Area (# sprinklers @ discharge pressure)	Layout	In-Rack Sprinkler Protection Criteria — Sprinkler Type/Nominal Orifice (gpm/psi$^{0.5}$)	Response/Nominal Temperature Rating	Discharge Flow (gpm)	Hose Stream Demand (gpm)	Water Supply Duration (hr)
30	20	ESFR-pendent K = 14.0	QR/Ordinary	12 @ 75 psi	Figure 6.3.2.7(d)	Spray K-8 or K-11.2	QR/Ordinary	45	250	1
		ESFR-pendent K = 16.8	QR/Ordinary	12 @ 52 psi	Figure 6.3.2.7(d)	Spray K-8 or K-11.2	QR/Ordinary	45	250	1
		ESFR-pendent K = 22.4	QR/Ordinary	12 @ 45 psi	Figure 6.3.2.7(d)	Spray K-8 or K-11.2	QR/Ordinary	45	250	1
		ESFR-pendent K = 25.2	QR/Ordinary	12 @ 25 psi	Figure 6.3.2.7(d)	Spray K-8 or K-11.2	QR/Ordinary	45	250	1
		Spray K ≥ 11.2	SR/High	0.6 gpm/ft² over 2000 ft²	Figure 6.3.2.7(d)	Spray K-8 or K-11.2	QR/Ordinary	45	500	2
		Spray K ≥ 8.0	SR/High	0.3 gpm/ft² over 2500 ft²	Figure 6.3.2.7(e)	Spray K-8 or K-11.2	QR/Ordinary	45	500	2
	25	ESFR-pendent K = 14.0	QR/Ordinary	12 @ 75 psi	Figure 6.3.2.7(e)	Spray K-8 or K-11.2	QR/Ordinary	45	250	1
		ESFR-pendent K = 16.8	QR/Ordinary	12 @ 52 psi	Figure 6.3.2.7(e)	Spray K-8 or K-11.2	QR/Ordinary	45	250	1
		ESFR-pendent K = 22.4	QR/Ordinary	12 @ 45 psi	Figure 6.3.2.7(e)	Spray K-8 or K-11.2	QR/Ordinary	45	250	1
		ESFR-pendent K = 25.2	QR/Ordinary	12 @ 25 psi	Figure 6.3.2.7(e)	Spray K-8 or K-11.2	QR/Ordinary	45	250	1
		Spray K ≥ 8.0	SR/High	0.3 gpm/ft² over 2500 ft²	Figure 6.3.2.7(e)	Spray K-8 or K-11.2	QR/Ordinary	45	500	2

QR: Quick response. SR: Standard response. ESFR: Early suppression fast response.
Note: See 6.3.2.9.1 for in-rack sprinkler design.

aerosol product storage area and shall meet the following requirements:

(1) The total floor area of the segregated Level 2 and Level 3 aerosol storage area(s) shall not exceed 15 percent of the total area of the warehouse, up to a maximum of 1,830 m² (20,000 ft²).
(2) The limits of the aerosol product storage area shall be clearly marked on the floor.
(3) The separation area shall be a minimum of 7.6 m (25 ft) and shall be maintained clear of all materials that have a commodity classification greater than Class III, according to NFPA 13, *Standard for the Installation of Sprinkler Systems*.
(4) The area of the design for the required ceiling sprinkler system shall extend 6 m (20 ft) beyond the segregated area.

6.3.5.4 Sprinkler protection shall be provided for segregated aerosol product storage areas in accordance with Table 6.3.2.7(a) through Table 6.3.2.7(l). Protection shall be provided for the highest level of aerosol products present.

6.3.5.5 An approved fire alarm system, meeting the requirements of Section 4.7, shall be provided throughout buildings used for the warehousing of segregated Level 2 or Level 3 aerosol products.

6.3.5.6 Activation of the fire alarm system required by 6.3.5.5 shall cause all fire doors or gates protecting openings in the enclosure surrounding the segregated aerosol product storage area to close automatically.

6.3.5.7 Storage of flammable and combustible liquids shall be separated from the segregated area by a minimum distance of 8 m (25 ft) or by the segregating wall.

6.3.6 Aerosol Warehouses.

6.3.6.1 Storage of Level 2 and Level 3 aerosol products in excess of the amounts permitted in 6.3.4 and 6.3.5 shall be located within an aerosol warehouse.

6.3.6.2 Aerosol warehouses shall be protected by automatic sprinkler systems in accordance with Table 6.3.2.7(a) through Table 6.3.2.7(l).

6.3.6.2.1 Protection shall be provided for the highest level of aerosol product present.

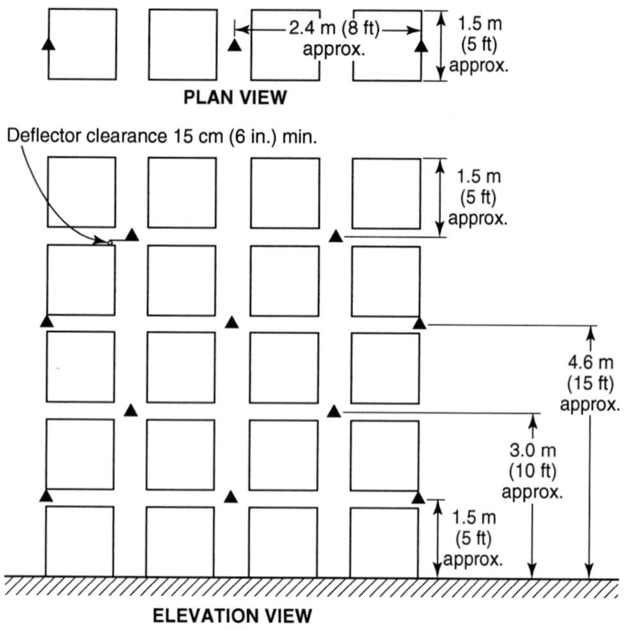

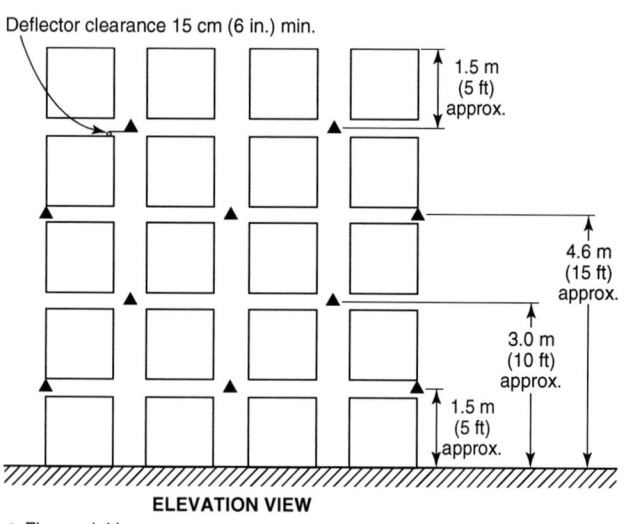

FIGURE 6.3.2.7(a) In-Rack Sprinkler Layout, Cartoned Level 2 and Level 3 Aerosols.

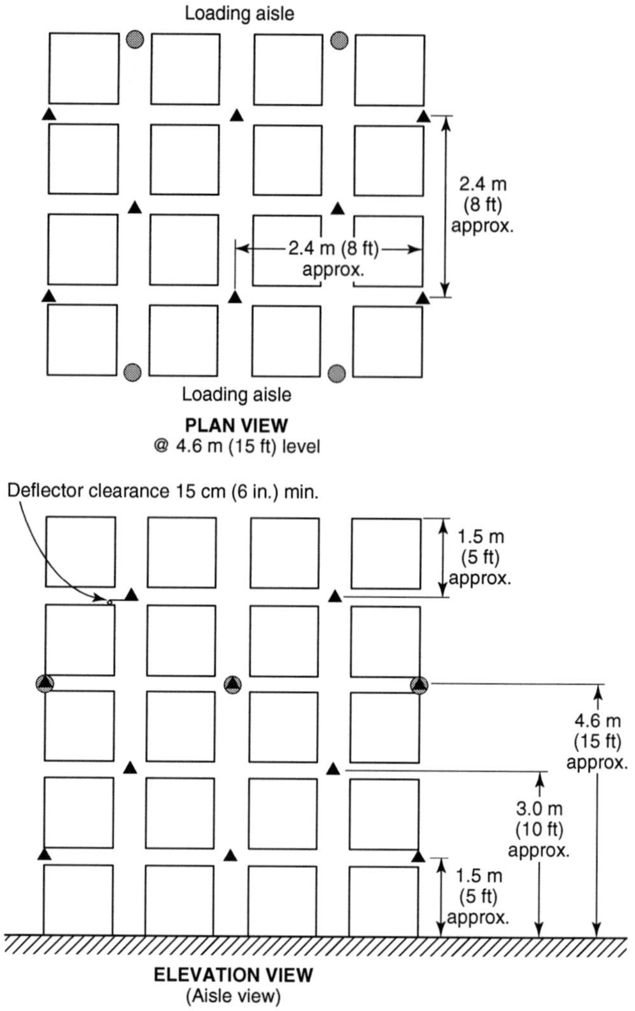

STORAGE IN WAREHOUSES AND STORAGE AREAS

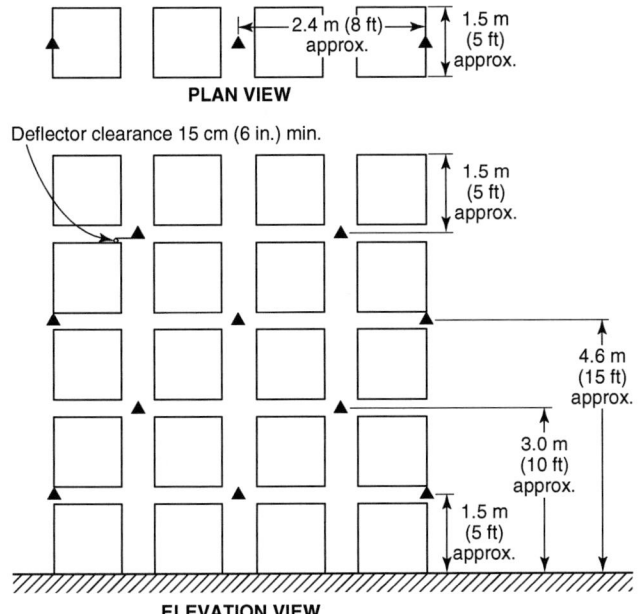

(1) Single Row Racks

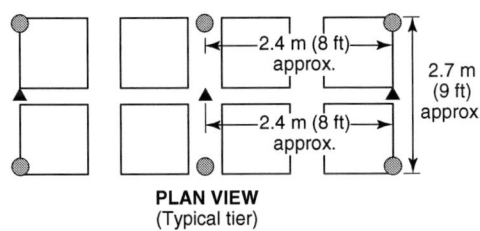

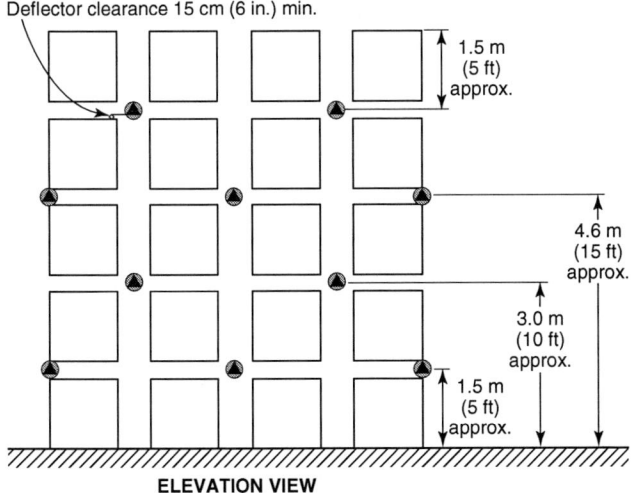

▲ Flue sprinkler ● Face sprinkler

Note: In-rack sprinklers must be staggered vertically; line up in-rack sprinklers with transverse flue spaces.

(2) Double Row Racks

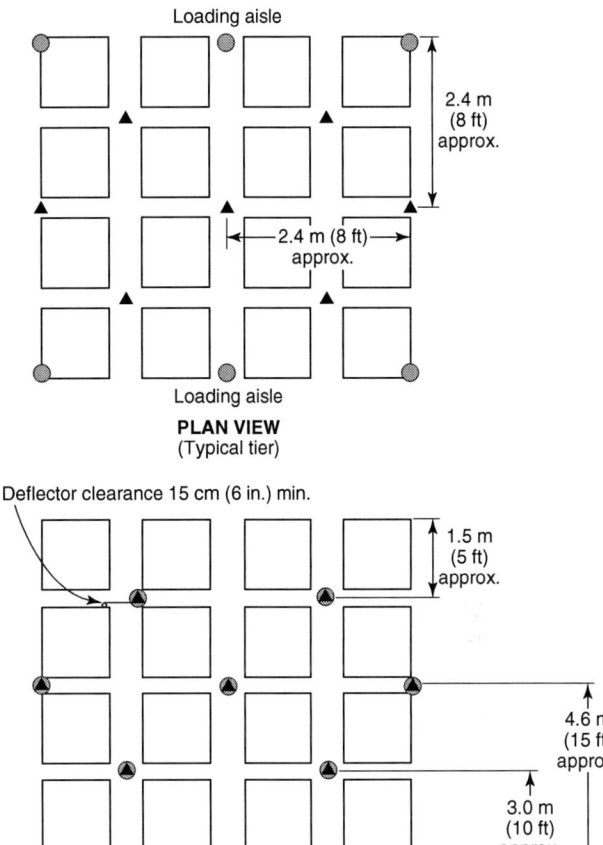

▲ Flue sprinkler ● Face sprinkler

Note: Line up in-rack sprinklers with transverse flue spaces; in-rack sprinklers must be staggered vertically and horizontally.

(3) Multiple Row Racks

FIGURE 6.3.2.7(b) In-Rack Sprinkler Layout, Cartoned Level 3 Aerosols.

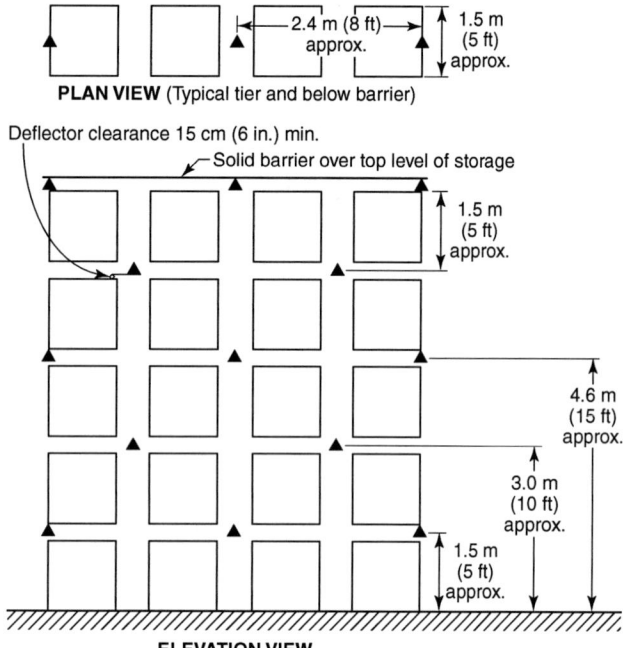

(1) Single Row Racks

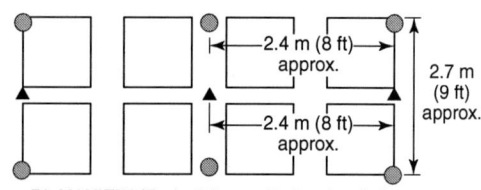

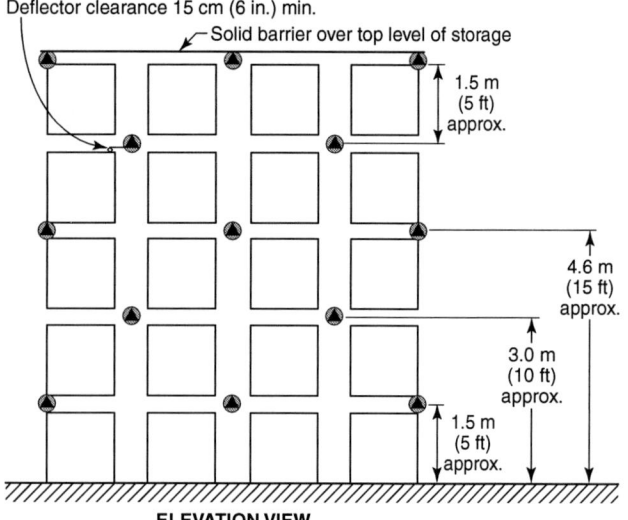

▲ Flue sprinkler ● Face sprinkler

Note: In-rack sprinklers must be staggered vertically; line up in-rack sprinklers with transverse flue spaces.

(2) Double Row Racks

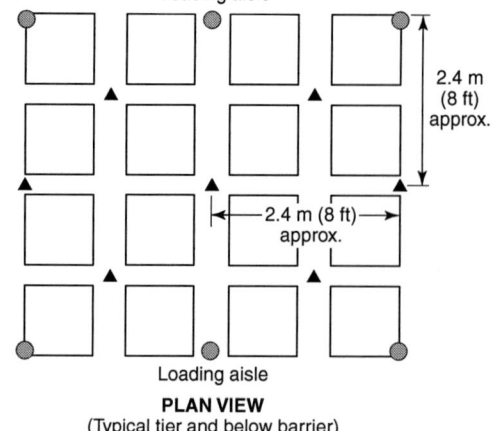

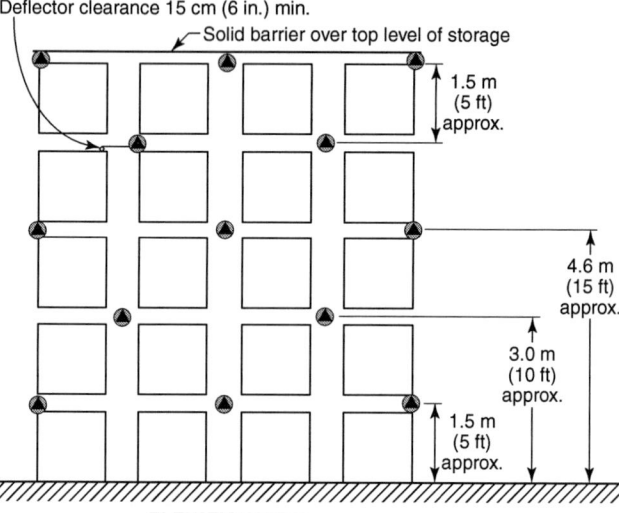

▲ Flue sprinkler ● Face sprinkler

Note: Line up in-rack sprinklers with transverse flue spaces; in-rack sprinklers must be staggered vertically and horizontally.

(3) Multiple Row Racks

FIGURE 6.3.2.7(c) In-Rack Sprinkler Layout, Cartoned Level 2 and Level 3 Aerosols, Clearance Greater Than 4.6 m (15 ft).

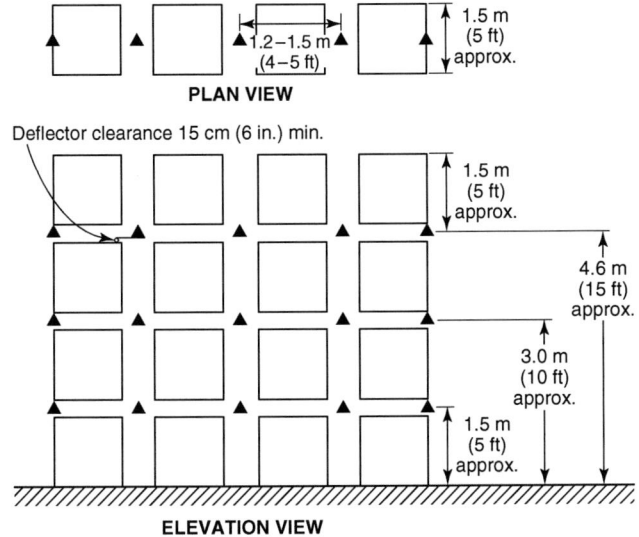

(1) Single Row Racks up to 6.1 m (20 ft) High Storage

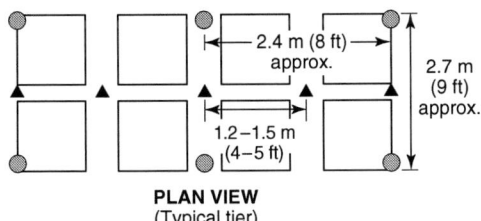

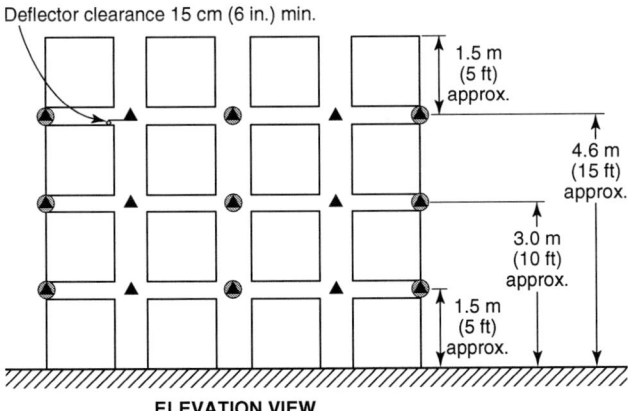

▲ Flue sprinkler ● Face sprinkler

Note: Face sprinklers are NOT staggered vertically; line up in-rack sprinklers with transverse flue spaces.

(2) Double Row Racks up to 6.1 m (20 ft) High Storage

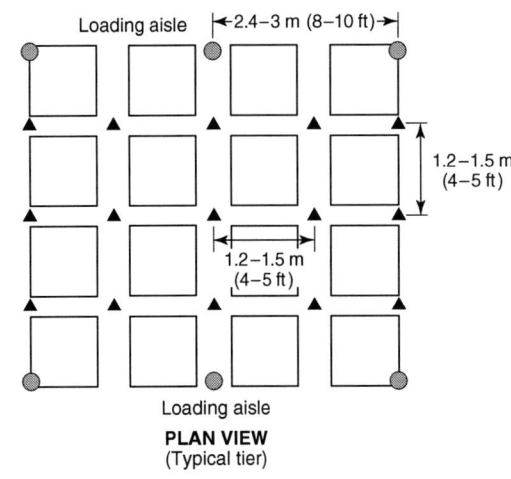

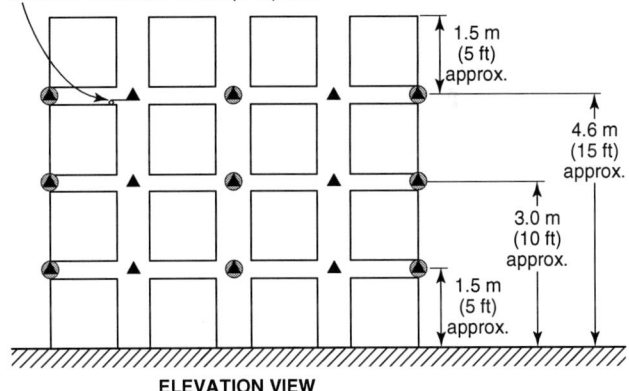

▲ Flue sprinkler ● Face sprinkler

Note: Face sprinklers are NOT staggered vertically; line up in-rack sprinklers with transverse flue spaces.

(3) Multiple Row Racks up to 6.1 m (20 ft) High Storage

FIGURE 6.3.2.7(d) In-Rack Sprinkler Layout, Uncartoned Level 2 and Level 3 Aerosols, Racks up to 6.1 m (20 ft) High Storage.

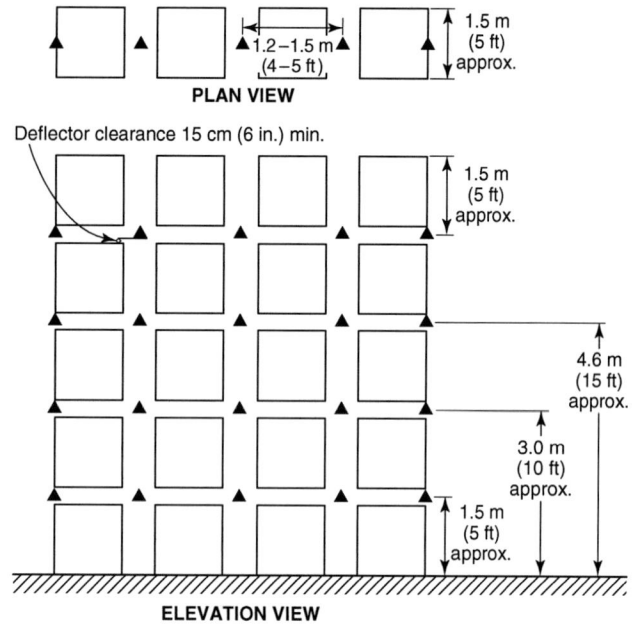

(1) Single Row Racks up to 7.6 m (25 ft) High Storage

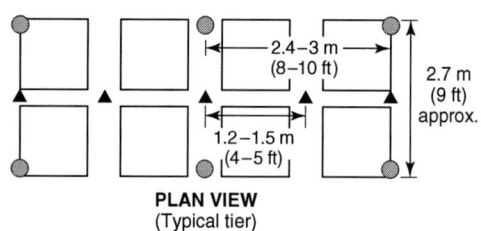

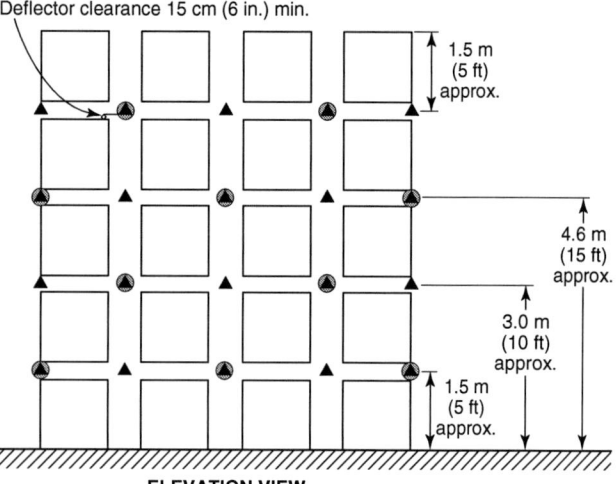

▲ Flue sprinkler ● Face sprinkler

Note: Face sprinklers must be staggered vertically; line up in-rack sprinklers with transverse flue spaces.

(2) Double Row Racks up to 7.6 m (25 ft) High Storage

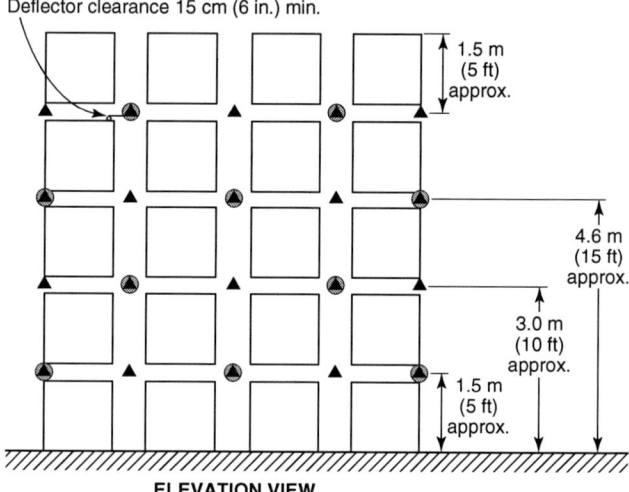

▲ Flue sprinkler ● Face sprinkler

Note: Line up in-rack sprinklers with transverse flue spaces; face sprinklers must be staggered vertically.

(3) Multiple Row Racks up to 7.6 m (25 ft) High Storage

FIGURE 6.3.2.7(e) In-Rack Sprinkler Layout, Uncartoned Level 2 and Level 3 Aerosols, Racks up to 7.6 m (25 ft) High Storage.

Table 6.3.5.3.1.1 Fire Protection Ratings for Fire Doors

Fire-Resistance Rating of Wall (hr)	Fire Protection Rating of Door (hr)
1	¾
2	1½
4	3*

*One fire door required on each side of interior openings for attached aerosol warehouses.

6.3.6.2.1.1 Subject to the approval of the AHJ, an unprotected aerosol warehouse shall be located a minimum of 30 m (100 ft) from exposed buildings or adjoining property that can be built upon if there is protection for exposures.

6.3.6.2.1.2 Where protection for exposures is not provided, a minimum 60 m (200 ft) distance is required.

6.3.6.3 Aerosol warehouses shall be separate, detached buildings or shall be separated from other occupancies by freestanding 4-hour fire walls, with communicating openings protected on each side by automatic-closing, listed 3-hour fire doors.

6.3.6.4 If the aerosol warehouse building is located more than 3 m (10 ft), but less than 15 m (50 ft), from an important building or line of adjoining property that can be built upon, the exposing wall shall have a fire resistance rating of at least 2 hours, with each opening protected with a listed 1½-hour fire door.

6.3.6.5 If the aerosol warehouse building is located 3 m (10 ft) or less from an important building or line of adjoining property that can be built upon, the exposing wall shall have a fire resistance rating of 4 hours, with each opening protected with a listed 3-hour fire door.

6.3.6.6 The total quantity of aerosols within an aerosol warehouse shall not be restricted.

6.3.6.7 Combustible commodities, other than flammable and combustible liquids, shall be permitted to be stored in an aerosol product warehouse, provided the warehouse is protected in accordance with Table 6.3.2.7(a) through Table 6.3.2.7(l), whichever is applicable.

6.3.6.7.1 Flammable and combustible liquids in metal containers of 0.9 L (1 qt) capacity or less shall be permitted to be stored in an aerosol product warehouse, provided the warehouse is protected in accordance with Table 6.3.2.7(e) through Table 6.3.2.7(l).

6.3.7 Storage of Aerosol Products in Inside Liquid Storage Areas, Liquid Storage Rooms, and Liquid Storage Control Areas.

6.3.7.1 Storage of aerosol products shall be permitted in inside liquid storage areas, liquid storage rooms, and liquid storage control areas of 47 m^2 (500 ft^2) or less that meet the requirements of NFPA 30, *Flammable and Combustible Liquids Code*, up to a maximum quantity of 454 kg (1000 lb) net weight of Level 2 aerosol products, or 227 kg (500 lb) net weight of Level 3 aerosol products, or 454 kg (1000 lb) net weight of combined Level 2 and Level 3 aerosol products.

6.3.7.2 Storage of aerosol products shall be permitted in inside liquid storage areas, liquid storage rooms, and liquid storage control areas of greater than 47 m^2 (500 ft^2) that meet the requirements of NFPA 30, *Flammable and Combustible Liquids Code*, up to a maximum quantity of 1135 kg (2500 lb) net weight of Level 2 aerosol products, or 454 kg (1000 lb) net weight of Level 3 aerosol products, or 1135 kg (2500 lb) net weight of combined Level 2 and Level 3 aerosol products.

6.3.7.3 Storage of aerosol products shall be permitted in inside liquid storage areas, liquid storage rooms, and liquid storage control areas up to a maximum of 2270 kg (5000 lb) net weight if the separate inside storage area is protected by an automatic sprinkler system that is designed in accordance with Table 6.3.2.7(a) through Table 6.3.2.7(l), whichever is applicable.

6.3.8 Storage of Aerosol Products in Liquid Warehouses. Storage shall be as defined in NFPA 30, *Flammable and Combustible Liquids Code*.

6.3.8.1 Storage of Level 2 and Level 3 aerosol products in a liquid warehouse, as defined in NFPA 30, *Flammable and Combustible Liquids Code*, shall be within a segregated area.

6.3.8.2 Storage of Level 2 and Level 3 aerosol products shall be in a segregated area that is separated from the rest of the warehouse by either interior walls or chain-link fencing, in accordance with the requirements of 6.3.8.2.2 or 6.3.8.2.3.

6.3.8.2.1 Where aerosol products are stored in a detached, unprotected liquid warehouse, as allowed by Chapter 13 of NFPA 30, *Flammable and Combustible Liquids Code*, the aerosol products shall not be required to be in a segregated area. Storage configuration shall meet the requirements of 6.3.2.17 through 6.3.2.19.

6.3.8.2.2 Interior walls shall have a fire resistance rating of 1 or 2 hours and shall be continuous from the floor to the underside of the roof deck.

6.3.8.2.2.1 Openings in these walls shall be protected with self-closing or automatic-closing listed fire door assemblies with fire protection ratings corresponding to the fire resistance rating of the wall as specified in Table 6.3.5.3.1.1.

(A) For interior walls having a fire resistance rating of 2 hours, the total floor area of the segregated Level 2 and Level 3 aerosol storage area(s) shall not exceed 25 percent of the total floor area of the warehouse, up to a maximum of 3,700 m^2 (40,000 ft^2).

(B) For interior walls having a fire resistance rating of 1 hour, the total floor area of the segregated Level 2 and Level 3 aerosol storage area(s) shall not exceed 20 percent of the total floor area of the warehouse, up to a maximum of 1,850 m^2 (30,000 ft^2).

(C) Spill control or drainage shall be provided to prevent the flow of liquid to within 2.4 m (8 ft) of the segregated area.

6.3.8.2.3 Chain-link fencing shall extend from the floor to the underside of the roof deck and shall meet the requirements of 6.3.8.2.3.1 through 6.3.8.2.3.8.

6.3.8.2.3.1 The total floor area of the segregated Level 2 and Level 3 aerosol storage area(s) shall not exceed 20 percent of the total floor area of the warehouse, up to a maximum of 1,850 m^2 (20,000 ft^2).

6.3.8.2.3.2* Fencing shall be not lighter than 2.9 mm (9 gauge) steel wire woven into a maximum 5 cm (2 in.) diamond mesh.

6.3.8.2.3.3 All storage outside the segregated storage area shall be kept at least 2.4 m (8 ft) from the fence.

6.3.8.2.3.4 Spill control or drainage shall be provided to prevent the flow of liquid to within 2.4 m (8 ft) of the segregated storage area.

6.3.8.2.3.5 The area that extends for 6 m (20 ft) beyond the segregated storage area shall be protected by an automatic sprinkler system designed in accordance with the requirements for storage of aerosol products, as specified by this code, or in accordance with the requirements for liquid storage, as specified in NFPA 30, *Flammable and Combustible Liquids Code*, whichever is the more restrictive.

6.3.8.2.3.6 All openings in the fencing shall be provided with self-closing or automatic-closing gates or shall be protected with a labyrinth arrangement.

6.3.8.2.3.7 Where automatic-closing gates are used, manual closure actuating devices shall be provided adjacent to the opening to allow for manual closure of the gates.

6.3.8.2.3.8 A minimum of two personnel exits shall be provided.

6.3.8.3 Sprinkler protection shall be provided for segregated aerosol product storage areas in accordance with Table 6.3.2.7(a) through Table 6.3.2.7(l). Protection shall be provided for the highest level of aerosol products present.

6.3.8.4 Fire doors or gates that lead into the segregated storage area shall be either self-closing or provided with automatic-closing devices that are activated by water flow or by an approved fire detection system.

6.3.9 Outdoor Storage.

6.3.9.1* Level 2 and Level 3 aerosol products that are stored outdoors shall be separated from important buildings or structures.

6.3.9.2 A minimum 15 m (50 ft) separation shall be maintained between Level 2 and Level 3 aerosol products and other combustible yard storage.

6.3.9.3 Temporary storage trailers shall be located a minimum of 15 m (50 ft) from buildings, any property line that can be built upon, and other unprotected or combustible yard storage. A maximum of two such trailers shall be permitted in any one storage group.

6.3.9.4 Storage shall meet all applicable requirements of NFPA 1, *Fire Code*.

Chapter 7 Mercantile Occupancies

7.1 Sales Display Areas — Aerosol Storage Not Exceeding 2.4 m (8 ft) High.

7.1.1 Level 1 aerosol products in sales display areas shall not be limited.

7.1.2 Level 2 and Level 3 aerosol products shall be removed from combustible cartons, or the cartons shall be display-cut, when located in sales display areas.

7.1.2.1 Cartoned display of Level 2 and Level 3 aerosol products shall be permitted, provided the area is protected in accordance with Table 6.3.2.7(a) through Table 6.3.2.7(l).

7.1.3 Level 2 and Level 3 aerosol products in sales display areas shall not exceed the maximum quantities given in 7.1.3.1 and 7.1.3.2 according to the protection provided.

7.1.3.1 In sales display areas that are nonsprinklered or whose sprinkler system does not meet the requirements of 7.1.3.2, the total aggregate quantity of Level 2 and Level 3 aerosol products and aerosol products in plastic containers shall not exceed 9.8 kg/m^2 (2 lb/ft^2) of total sales display area, up to the quantities specified in Table 7.1.3.1.

Table 7.1.3.1 Maximum Quantity per Floor of Level 2 and Level 3 Aerosol Products and Aerosol Products in Plastic Containers

Floor	Max. Net Weight per Floor kg	lb
Basement	Not Permitted	
Ground	1135	2500
Upper	227	500

7.1.3.1.1 No single 3 m × 3 m (10 ft × 10 ft) section of sales display area shall contain an aggregate quantity of more than 454 kg (1000 lb) net weight of Level 2 and Level 3 aerosol products and aerosol products in plastic containers.

7.1.3.2 In sales display areas that are sprinklered in accordance with NFPA 13, *Standard for the Installation of Sprinkler Systems*, for at least Ordinary Hazard (Group 2) occupancies, the total aggregate quantity of Level 2 and Level 3 aerosol products shall not exceed 9.8 kg/m^2 (2 lb/ft^2) of total sales display area.

7.1.3.2.1 No single 3 m × 3 m (10 ft × 10 ft) section of sales display area shall contain an aggregate quantity of more than 454 kg (1000 lb) net weight of Level 2 and Level 3 aerosol products.

7.1.4 Level 2 and Level 3 aerosol products shall be securely stacked to not more than 1.8 m (6 ft) high from base to top of the storage array unless on fixed shelving.

7.1.4.1 Shelving shall be of stable construction and storage shall not exceed 2.4 m (8 ft) in height.

7.2 Sales Display Areas — Aerosol Storage Exceeding 2.4 m (8 ft) High.

7.2.1 Storage and display of Level 1 aerosol products in sales display areas shall not be limited.

7.2.2 Uncartoned or display-cut (case-cut) Level 2 and Level 3 aerosol products that are stored for display no more than 1.8 m (6 ft) above the floor shall be permitted where protection is installed in accordance with 7.2.3, based on the highest level of aerosol product in the array and the packaging method of the storage above 1.8 m (6 ft).

7.2.3 Protection.

7.2.3.1 The storage and display of Level 2 and Level 3 aerosol products in metal containers only shall be protected in accordance with Table 6.3.2.7(a) through Table 6.3.2.7(l), whichever is applicable.

7.2.3.1.1 Where in-rack sprinklers are required by Table 6.3.2.7(e) through Table 6.3.2.7(l) and where the Level 2 and Level 3 aerosol products are stored for display below the 1.8 m (6 ft) level, the first tier of in-rack sprinklers shall be installed above the display, but no more than 1.8 m (6 ft) above the floor level.

7.2.3.2 Noncombustible draft curtains shall extend down a minimum of 0.61 m (2 ft) from the ceiling and shall be installed at the interface between ordinary and high-temperature sprinklers.

7.2.4 Storage and display of Level 2 and Level 3 aerosol products shall not exceed 4,540 kg (10,000 lb) net weight within any 2,323 m² (25,000 ft²) of sales display area.

7.2.4.1 Level 2 and Level 3 aerosol product display areas shall be separated from each other by a minimum of 7.6 m (25 ft).

7.2.5 The area of the design for the required ceiling sprinkler system shall extend 6 m (20 ft) beyond the Level 2 and Level 3 aerosol display and storage area.

7.2.6 Storage and display of Level 2 and Level 3 aerosol products shall be separated from the storage of flammable and combustible liquids by a minimum distance of 7.6 m (25 ft) or by a segregating wall or noncombustible barrier.

7.2.6.1 Where Level 2 and Level 3 aerosol products are stored within 7.6 m (25 ft) of flammable and combustible liquids, beneath the noncombustible barrier shall be liquidtight at the floor to prevent spilled liquids from flowing beneath the aerosol products.

7.2.7 The sales display area shall meet the requirements for mercantile occupancies in NFPA *101, Life Safety Code.*

7.3 Back Stock Storage Areas.

7.3.1 Where back stock areas are separated from sales display areas by construction having a minimum 1-hour fire resistance rating, storage of Level 2 and Level 3 aerosol products shall meet the requirements of Chapter 6.

7.3.2 Where back stock areas are not separated from sales display areas by construction having a minimum 1-hour fire resistance rating, the quantity of Level 2 and Level 3 aerosol products in back stock areas shall be included in the total allowable quantities specified in 7.1.3 or 7.2.4.

7.3.2.1 Protection shall be provided in accordance with 7.2.3.

7.3.3 An additional quantity of Level 2 and Level 3 aerosol products, up to a maximum of 227 kg (500 lb) net weight, shall be permitted in back stock areas where the additional quantities are stored in flammable liquid storage cabinets that meet the requirements of Section 9.5 of NFPA 30, *Flammable and Combustible Liquids Code.*

7.3.4 Storage of Level 2 and Level 3 aerosol products in separate, inside flammable liquids storage rooms shall meet the requirements of 6.3.7.

7.4 Special Protection Design.

7.4.1 Section 7.4 prescribes a special protection design methodology for the storage and display of Level 2 and Level 3 aerosol products in double-row racks. Protection shall be in accordance with Table 7.4.1, Figure 7.4.1, and 7.2.3.2, 7.2.4, and Section 7.4.

7.4.2 Storage and display of Level 2 and Level 3 aerosol products shall be in cartons.

Table 7.4.1 Protection of Single, Double-Row Display/Rack Storage of Level 2 and Level 3 Aerosols with In-Rack Sprinklers

Maximum Ceiling Height	Maximum Storage Height	Ceiling Sprinkler Type and Arrangement	Clearance Storage to Sprinklers	Ceiling Design	In-Rack Sprinkler Type and Arrangement	In-Rack Design	Duration (hr)
9.1 m (30 ft)	4.8 m (16 ft)	ESFR (K = 25.2), Ordinary Temperature, 9.3 m² (100 ft²) maximum spacing	Up to 4.6 m (15 ft)	12 sprinklers @15 psi	Quick-response, ordinary temperature, K = 11.2 orifice size pendent sprinklers, maximum 127 mm (50 in.) on center spacing located 2.4 m (8 ft) above floor at each rack face and in longitudinal flue space, if a double row rack. A barrier shall be located directly over level of in-rack sprinklers.	56 gpm per sprinkler minimum based on operation of hydraulically most remote 12 sprinklers	2
		ESFR (K = 14) Ordinary Temperature, 9.3 m² (100 ft²) maximum spacing		12 sprinklers @ 50 psi			

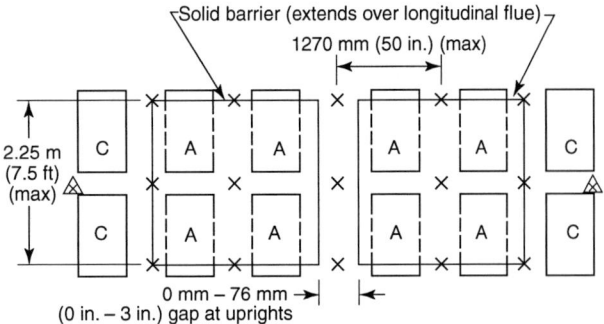

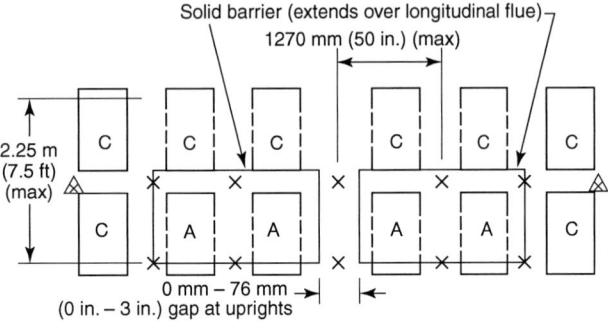

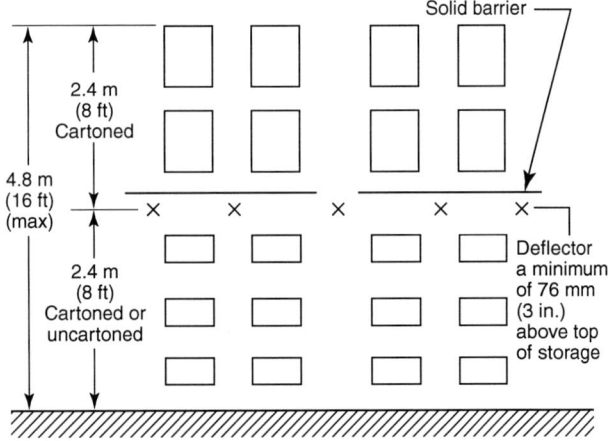

× In-rack sprinkler, K = 11.2, ordinary, OR
△ Continue in-rack sprinklers for protection of flammable liquids and combustible liquids
A Level 2 and Level 3 aerosols
C Flammable liquids, combustible liquids, and ordinary combustibles
(See 7.4.7 and 7.4.8.)

FIGURE 7.4.1 Special Protection for Level 2 and Level 3 Aerosol Products in Double-Row Racks.

7.4.2.1 Containers of Level 2 and Level 3 aerosol products that are stored or displayed no more than 2.4 m (8 ft) above the floor shall be permitted to be uncartoned or in display-cut cartons.

7.4.3 Storage and display of Level 2 and Level 3 aerosol products shall be on open racks or wire mesh shelves.

7.4.4 Rack storage shall be arranged so that a minimum aisle width of 2.3 m (7.5 ft) is maintained between rows of rack and adjacent solid piled or palletized storage.

7.4.5 Nominal 76 mm (3 in.) transverse flue spaces at rack uprights and nominal 152 mm (6 in.) longitudinal flue spaces shall be provided.

7.4.6 Horizontal barriers of plywood [minimum 10 mm (⅜ in.) thickness] or sheet metal (minimum 22 gauge) and in-rack sprinklers shall be installed in accordance with Table 7.4.1 and Figure 7.4.1.

7.4.6.1 For double-row racks with aerosol product storage on only one side, the horizontal barrier shall extend over the longitudinal flue space in accordance with Plan View 2 of Figure 7.4.1.

7.4.7 Ordinary combustibles (Class I, II, III, and IV, and plastic commodities) shall be permitted to be stored adjacent to Level 2 and Level 3 aerosol products, provided that the ordinary combustibles are protected in accordance with NFPA 13, *Standard for the Installation of Sprinkler Systems*.

7.4.8 Flammable and combustible liquids (Class IB, IC, II, IIIA, and IIIB) in one-gallon metal relieving and nonrelieving style containers and five-gallon metal relieving style containers shall be permitted to be stored adjacent to Level 2 and Level 3 aerosol products *(see Figure 7.4.1)*, provided that the sprinkler protection for the flammable and combustible liquids is in accordance with NFPA 30, *Flammable and Combustible Liquids Code*.

Chapter 8 Operations and Maintenance

8.1 Means of Egress. Means of egress and exits shall be maintained in accordance with NFPA *101, Life Safety Code*.

8.2 Powered Industrial Trucks.

8.2.1 The use and selection of powered industrial trucks shall comply with NFPA 505, *Fire Safety Standard for Powered Industrial Trucks Including Type Designations, Areas of Use, Conversions, Maintenance, and Operations*.

8.2.2 Only trained and authorized operators shall be allowed to operate powered industrial trucks.

8.2.3 Operator training shall be equivalent to that specified by ANSI/ASME B56.1, *Safety Standard for Low-Lift and High-Lift Trucks*.

8.2.4 Loads.

8.2.4.1 If the type of load handled presents a hazard of backward falls, the powered industrial truck shall be equipped with a vertical load backrest extension.

8.2.4.2 For loads that are elevated above the mast of the truck, the backrest extension shall reach at least halfway into the uppermost pallet load.

8.3 Control of Ignition Sources.

8.3.1 Sources of Ignition.

8.3.1.1 In areas where flammable gases or flammable vapors might be present, precautions shall be taken to prevent ignition by eliminating or controlling sources of ignition. Sources of ignition include, but are not limited to, the following:

(1) Open flames
(2) Lightning
(3) Hot surfaces
(4) Radiant heat

(5) Smoking
(6) Cutting and welding
(7) Spontaneous ignition
(8) Frictional heat or sparks
(9) Static electricity
(10) Electrical arcs and sparks
(11) Stray currents
(12) Ovens, furnaces, and other heating equipment
(13) Automotive vehicles
(14) Material-handling equipment

8.3.2 Smoking shall be strictly prohibited, except in designated smoking areas.

8.3.3* Welding, cutting, and similar spark-producing operations shall not be permitted in areas that contain aerosol products, until a written permit authorizing the work has been issued.

8.3.3.1 The permit shall be issued by a person in authority following an inspection of the area to assure that proper precautions have been taken and will be followed until completion of the work.

8.4 Aisles. Storage in aisles shall be prohibited so as to permit access for fire fighting, salvage, and removal of stored commodities.

8.5 Waste Disposal.

8.5.1 Filled or partly filled aerosol containers shall be separated from all other rubbish and trash.

8.5.1.1 Filled or partly filled aerosol containers shall be placed in noncombustible waste containers.

8.5.2 Filled or partly filled aerosol containers shall not be disposed of in compactors, balers, or incinerators that crush the container or heat its contents.

8.5.2.1 Equipment and facilities that are specifically designed for the disposal of aerosol containers shall be permitted to dispose of filled or partly filled aerosol containers.

8.6 Inspection and Maintenance.

8.6.1 A written and documented preventive maintenance program shall be developed for equipment, machinery, and processes that are critical to fire-safe operation of the facility.

8.6.2 Critical detection systems and their components, emergency trips and interlocks, alarms, and safety shutdown systems shall be inspected on a regularly scheduled basis, and any deficiencies shall be immediately corrected.

8.6.2.1 Items in this inspection schedule shall include, but are not limited to, the following:

(1) Gas detection systems
(2) Deflagration suppression systems
(3) Deflagration vent systems
(4) Ventilation and local exhaust systems
(5) Propellant charging room door interlocks
(6) Process safety devices
(7) Fire alarm systems

8.6.3 Maintenance. [**68**:11.9]

8.6.3.1 Deflagration vent closure maintenance shall be performed after every act of nature or process upset condition to ensure that the closure has not been physically damaged and there are no obstructions including but not limited to snow, ice, water, mud, or process material that could lessen or impair the efficiency of the vent closure. [**68**:11.9.1]

8.6.3.2 An inspection shall be performed in accordance with 11.4.4 of NFPA 68, *Standard on Explosion Protection by Deflagration Venting*, after every process maintenance turnaround. [**68**:11.9.2]

8.6.3.3 If process material has a tendency to adhere to the vent closure, the vent closure shall be cleaned periodically to maintain vent efficiency. [**68**:11.9.3]

8.6.3.4 Process interlocks, if provided, shall be verified. [**68**:11.9.4]

8.6.3.5 Known potential ignition sources shall be inspected and maintained. [**68**:11.9.5]

8.6.3.6 Records shall be kept of any maintenance and repairs performed. [**68**:11.9.6]

8.7* Static Electricity. All process equipment and piping involved in the transfer of flammable liquids or gases shall be connected to a static-dissipating earth ground system to prevent accumulations of static charge.

Annex A Explanatory Material

Annex A is not a part of the requirements of this NFPA document but is included for informational purposes only. This annex contains explanatory material, numbered to correspond with the applicable text paragraphs.

A.1.1.2 See NFPA 58, *Liquefied Petroleum Gas Code.*

A.1.1.4 This code does not apply to products that can be dispensed as aerosolized sprays that are not packaged in aerosol containers as defined in 3.3.2. This code is not applicable to other applications such as industrial spray adhesives that are dispensed from large [18.9 L–475 L (5–125 gal)] pressurized gas cylinders. There is no assurance that the protection specified in this code will be adequate.

A.1.2 This code provides minimum acceptable requirements for fire prevention and protection in facilities that manufacture and store aerosol products and in mercantile occupancies where aerosol products are displayed and sold. As explained in A.5.1, the hazards presented by each stage of the manufacturing process will vary, depending on the flammability of the base product and on the flammability of the propellant. Considerable judgment will be required of the designer and of the authority having jurisdiction to provide an adequate level of fire protection. *(See also Annex B, Mechanism of Fire Growth in Aerosol Containers.)*

A.1.4 This section should not be interpreted as discouraging the upgrading of existing aerosol manufacturing or storage facilities. Improvements to fire protection systems in existing facilities should be allowed without requiring retroactive compliance with all of the requirements of this code. It is the intent of this code, however, that major renovations to such a facility should meet, to the greatest extent practical, the requirements of this code.

A.1.7 Tests have shown that aerosol products in plastic containers with a heat of combustion of 10.5 kJ/g have been adequately protected as determined by fire tests. See Section B.5 for a description of the aerosol testing in plastic containers.

A.3.2.1 Approved. The National Fire Protection Association does not approve, inspect, or certify any installations, procedures, equipment, or materials; nor does it approve or evaluate testing laboratories. In determining the acceptability of installations, procedures, equipment, or materials, the authority having jurisdiction may base acceptance on compliance with NFPA or other appropriate standards. In the absence of such standards, said authority may require evidence of proper installation, procedure, or use. The authority having jurisdiction may also refer to the listings or labeling practices of an organization that is concerned with product evaluations and is thus in a position to determine compliance with appropriate standards for the current production of listed items.

A.3.2.2 Authority Having Jurisdiction (AHJ). The phrase "authority having jurisdiction," or its acronym AHJ, is used in NFPA documents in a broad manner, since jurisdictions and approval agencies vary, as do their responsibilities. Where public safety is primary, the authority having jurisdiction may be a federal, state, local, or other regional department or individual such as a fire chief; fire marshal; chief of a fire prevention bureau, labor department, or health department; building official; electrical inspector; or others having statutory authority. For insurance purposes, an insurance inspection department, rating bureau, or other insurance company representative may be the authority having jurisdiction. In many circumstances, the property owner or his or her designated agent assumes the role of the authority having jurisdiction; at government installations, the commanding officer or departmental official may be the authority having jurisdiction.

A.3.2.3 Code. The decision to designate a standard as a "code" is based on such factors as the size and scope of the document, its intended use and form of adoption, and whether it contains substantial enforcement and administrative provisions.

A.3.3.1 Aerosol. The base product can be dispensed from the container in such form as a mist, spray, foam, gel, or aerated powder.

A.3.3.2 Aerosol Container. Maximum sizes, minimum strengths, and other critical limitations for aerosol containers are set by the U.S. Department of Transportation (49 CFR). These regulations ensure that aerosol products can be safely transported in interstate commerce. Aerosol products are generally classified as Other Regulated Materials — Class D (ORM-D). A cutaway drawing of a typical aerosol container is shown in Figure A.3.3.2. Labeling of aerosol products, including precautionary language for flammability and other hazards, is regulated by a number of federal authorities, including the Consumer Product Safety Commission, the Food and Drug Administration, the Environmental Protection Agency, the Occupational Safety and Health Administration, and the Federal Trade Commission.

Additional information on the labeling of aerosol products is given in Annex D, Flammability Labeling of Aerosol Products.

A.3.3.3 Aerosol Propellant. The flammable propellant is generally a hydrocarbon gas, such as butane, isobutane, propane, and various blends of these gases. Systems that generate a propellant gas are included in this definition.

A.3.3.5 Base Product (Concentrate). The base product contains the active ingredient of the aerosol product.

A.3.3.9 Cold Filling. Reprinted with permission from ASTM D 3064, *Standard Definitions of Terms and Nomenclature Relating to Aerosol Products.*

A.3.3.22.1 Combustible Liquid. Combustible liquids are further subclassified as follows:

(1) Class II Liquid — Any liquid that has a flash point at or above 37.8°C (100°F) and below 60°C (140°F)
(2) Class III Liquid — Any liquid that has a flash point at or above 60°C (140°F)
  (a) Class IIIA Liquid — Any liquid that has a flash point at or above 60°C (140°F), but below 93°C (200°F)
  (b) Class IIIB Liquid — Any liquid that has a flash point at or above 93°C (200°F) [30:4.3.2]

A.3.3.22.2 Flammable Liquid. Flammable liquids are further subclassified according to the following:

(1) Class IA Liquid — Any liquid that has a flash point below 22.8°C (73°F) and a boiling point below 37.8°C (100°F)
(2) Class IB Liquid — Any liquid that has a flash point below 22.8°C (73°F) and a boiling point at or above 37.8°C (100°F)
(3) Class IC Liquid — Any liquid that has a flash point at or above 22.8°C (73°F), but below 37.8°C (100°F) [30:4.3.1]

A.3.3.24 Net Weight. Label weight should always be used for calculation of total net weight. When dealing with limited quantities of aerosols, the total net weight is the sum of the individual container net weights.

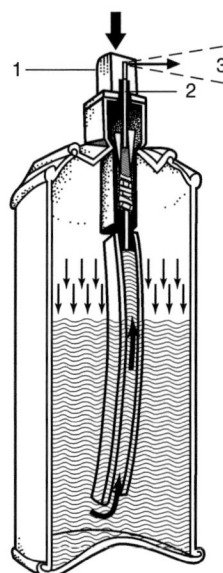

FIGURE A.3.3.2 Aerosol Can (Cutaway View). When the plunger (1) is pressed, a hole in the valve (2) allows a pressurized mixture of product and propellant (3) to flow through the plunger's exit orifice. *[Source: Fire Protection Handbook, 19th edition]*

For example, if a small retail display area contains 100 198-g (100 7-oz) containers, 100 284-g (140 10-oz) containers, and 100 454-g (180 16-oz) containers, the total net weight is calculated as follows:

$$100 \text{ cans} \times \frac{198 \text{ g}}{\text{can}} = 19.8 \text{ kg}$$

$$140 \text{ cans} \times \frac{284 \text{ g}}{\text{can}} = 39.8 \text{ kg}$$

$$180 \text{ cans} \times \frac{454 \text{ g}}{\text{can}} = 81.7 \text{ kg}$$

Total = 141.3 kg

$$\left(\begin{array}{l} 100 \text{ cans} \times \dfrac{7 \text{ oz/can}}{16 \text{ oz/lb}} = \dfrac{700}{16} = 43.75 \text{ lb} \\ 140 \text{ cans} \times \dfrac{10 \text{ oz/can}}{16 \text{ oz/lb}} = \dfrac{1400}{16} = 87.5 \text{ lb} \\ 180 \text{ cans} \times \dfrac{16 \text{ oz/can}}{16 \text{ oz/lb}} = \dfrac{2880}{16} = 180 \text{ lb} \\ \text{Total} = 311 \text{ lb} \end{array} \right)$$

When dealing with larger quantities of product, the number of cases per pallet and the number of units per case also enter into the calculation.

For example, if a general-purpose warehouse contains 20 pallets of a product with a label weight of 340 g (12 oz), and there are 12 units per case, and 75 cases per pallet, the total net weight calculation is as follows:

$$\frac{340 \text{ g/unit}}{1000 \text{ g/kg}} \times 12 \text{ units/case} \times 75 \text{ cases/pallet} \\ \times 20 \text{ pallets} = 6120 \text{ kg}$$

$$\left[\begin{array}{l} \dfrac{12 \text{ oz/unit}}{16 \text{ oz/lb}} \times 12 \text{ units/case} \times 75 \text{ cases/pallet} \\ \times 20 \text{ pallets} = 13{,}500 \text{ lb} \end{array} \right]$$

A.3.3.28 Rack. For additional information, see NFPA 13, *Standard for the Installation of Sprinkler Systems*.

A.3.3.31.2 Face Sprinklers. All face sprinklers should be located within the rack structure. The flue spaces are generally created by the arrangement of the racks. Walkways should not be considered flue spaces.

A.3.4.2 Button Tipper (Actuator Placer). This operation sometimes releases small quantities of the container contents to the atmosphere.

A.3.4.6 Propellant Charging Room (Gas House, Gassing Room). The customary arrangement of equipment in a propellant charging room includes one or two propellant fillers and a high pressure propellant charging pump(s), if required. Occasionally, the vacuum pump will also be located in the propellant charging room, especially if one of the propellant fillers is an under-the-cup filler. The fillers have guard enclosures to prevent operator contact with mechanical hazards of the machine and to also protect from flying debris if a can ruptures or is thrown from the machine by a jam.

The filling machine enclosure is normally constructed of a permeable material, such as wire mesh, of sufficient strength to confine debris or loose cans, as necessary, but will allow complete ventilation of the machine. The wire mesh design works in conjunction with the propellant charging room ventilation system to completely dilute and remove propellant routinely released at the point where the filling head disengages from the aerosol container. It also allows propellant from incidental leaks on the machine to be swept into the ventilation stream and safely removed. In addition, the wire mesh allows the propellant charging room deflagration detection and suppression system to function effectively, since it does not block detection of the deflagration and the distribution of the suppression media.

Local ventilation can be provided at the head/container disengagement point to more efficiently remove propellant vapors at the source of release. See 5.4.2 to determine ventilation rate requirements. Local ventilation can replace up to 75 percent of the required ventilation for the propellant charging room; however, the propellant charging room ventilation is not permitted to be less than one air change per minute.

The basic requirements of this code pertain to this customary arrangement and design of the propellant charging room and associated equipment. Further design considerations are possible, but will require the application of sound design principles, testing, and technical documentation approved by the authority having jurisdiction to ensure safe operation. One example of further design considerations that fall outside of the basic requirements of this code is a propellant filling machine guard enclosure constructed of nonpermeable materials. Design consideration for such an arrangement should include proper ventilation and gas detection within the enclosure to prevent accumulation of propellant above safe LEL percentage limits, deflagration venting that does not endanger the operator, deflagration detection and suppression within the enclosure, and damage-limiting construction to prevent violent rupture of the enclosure in the event of a deflagration. In small enclosures, even suppressed deflagrations can result in significant pressure build-up due to the ratio of the volume of expanding gases with respect to the volume of the enclosed space, plus the added volume of the suppression media and compressed gas.

A.3.4.7 Propellant Filler (Gasser, Propellant Charger). Typically, it is one of two types: one adds the propellant through the crimped valve assembly; the other adds the propellant around the uncrimped valve assembly. The propellant is either a liquid, a gas, or both, during this filling operation.

A.3.4.11 Test Bath (Hot Tank, Water Bath). The test might be required by the U.S. Department of Transportation (49 CFR) to verify container strength and to detect leaks. Usually, the containers are heated to attain a pressure that is equal to the product's pressure at an equilibrium temperature.

A.5.1 The hazards relative to each manufacturing operation will depend on the flammability of both the base products and the propellant. Information on the properties of liquefied petroleum gases, including safe handling and storage, is found in NFPA 58, *Liquefied Petroleum Gas Code*. Information on the handling and storage of flammable and combustible liquids is found in NFPA 30, *Flammable and Combustible Liquids Code*.

An example of an aerosol product that is not flammable or combustible, and, therefore, not covered by this chapter, is whipped cream: the base product is a water-based material and the propellant is nitrous oxide, which is nonflammable.

A.5.3 It is essential that any flammable propellant charging room be designed by qualified professionals.

A.5.3.4.1 Aerosol-filling rooms that utilize flammable propellants have an inherent deflagration hazard. The hazard severity will depend upon the volume and speed of the accidental flammable gas release. The worst case explosion potential involves filling more than 10 percent of room volume with a flammable gas–air mixture.

The ignition of this flammable mixture will result in a significant pressure rise, the production of hot combustion gases, and flame. It is essential that the design of the room or building is proper for this type of event; otherwise failure of the room/building and/or roof could result from the uncontrolled release of the hot combustion gases, flames, and pressure. Damage-limiting construction is the best available technology for this type of event, which consists of a combination of pressure relieving deflagration venting and pressure-resistant construction. *(See NFPA 68, Standard on Explosion Protection by Deflagration Venting.)*

In certain cases, existing facilities could be difficult and extremely costly to retrofit with adequate damage-limiting construction. The protection performance goal in these cases is to limit the deflagration to the room of origin. The options available for controlling a deflagration in such facilities are limited. NFPA 69, *Standard on Explosion Prevention Systems*, provides some possible approaches that are aimed at either preventing deflagration (e.g., reducing oxygen concentrations, or reducing fuel concentration) or trying to limit the effects of a deflagration (e.g., deflagration suppression, deflagration pressure containment). The most commonly used approach involves use of a deflagration suppression system. Deflagration suppression systems are most likely to be effective when smaller gas releases are involved. The use of deflagration suppression systems is advised since the personnel protection benefits against a deflagration resulting from small flammable gas–air mixtures cannot be underestimated.

A.5.4.1 For further information, see NFPA 91, *Standard for Exhaust Systems for Air Conveying of Vapors, Gases, Mists, and Noncombustible Particulate Solids*.

A.5.4.2(D) Adequate ventilation of flammable propellant charging and pump rooms is necessary to maintain these rooms at a safe level, well below the lower explosive limit (LEL) of the propellant being used. The internal volume of these rooms should be as small as practical to minimize the capital and operating costs of the ventilation system, as well as the cost of heating and conditioning the required make-up air. The formula given in 5.4.2(D) is used to determine the required ventilation flow rate. In no case should the required ventilation be less than one air change per minute. The following are some considerations to take into account when using the formula:

(1) The LEL used in the calculation should be that of the most flammable propellant gas used. Normally, this will be isobutane (propellant A-31), which has an LEL of 1.8 percent in air at 21°C (70°F). Butane has the same LEL. All other flammable propellants have LELs that are higher. Thus, the two isomeric butanes are considered the most hazardous propellants, and the ventilation system is normally designed based on their use.

(2) The volume of vapor produced by one liter of propellant determines the quantity of saturated vapor that the ventilation system must handle, based on the volumetric flow rate of the propellant through the system. For isobutane, this factor is 0.23 m^3 of vapor per liter (30.77 ft^3 of vapor per gallon), at 21°C (70°F) and sea level conditions.

(3) The LEL design level is an arbitrary decimal fraction. This establishes the maximum amount of vapor concentration that the ventilation system will handle and is, in effect, a percentage of the LEL. Since combustible gas detection systems are set to alarm at 20 percent of the LEL and operational shutdown is set at 40 percent of the LEL, it is recommended that the design level not exceed 10 percent of the LEL. In other words, *DL* in the equation should not exceed 0.10.

(4) *R* as used in the equation represents an estimate of how much propellant is lost from the equipment under normal operating conditions, plus 20 percent for occasional leaks. These losses are due to minor seal and hose leakage and minor loss from the equipment as it is operating. This number is calculated as follows:

$$R = \left(\frac{1 \text{ gal}}{3785 \text{ cc}}\right) \times (\text{cc loss per can}) \times (\text{cans per minute}) \times (\text{safety factor})$$

The following considerations should be taken into account when using the above formula.

Loss per container. This is the maximum quantity of propellant that is expected to be lost during the propellant-filling operation and will depend on the type of filling mode used. Some propellant fillers will release 3.0 cubic centimeters (cc) per container per filling station.

Some propellant fillers will fill each container several times from separate filling stations. In this case, the loss per container will be the loss per fill multiplied by the number of fills per container.

Some filling operations require the use of two different fillers. An example is aerosol antiperspirant, which is filled using an under-the-cup filler, followed by a through-the-valve filler. The second filler injects a relatively small quantity of propellant, primarily to flush the viscous base product out of the aerosol diptube. For these systems, the combined release amounts to about 4.0 cc per container.

In other systems, different propellants are added at separate filling stations. This eliminates the need for propellant blending equipment or blend holding tanks. The manufacturer of the filling equipment should be consulted for an estimate of the expected losses during filling.

Cans per minute. This is the maximum production rate for the entire propellant charging room. The ventilation system needs to be designed to handle the expected losses from the highest number of cans that can foreseeably be filled per minute, based on a 10- to 20-minute reference period. The average rate per shift should not be used, since the average rate will always be lower than the maximum production rate by 10 percent to 25 percent. If there are multiple fill lines, the maximum production rates need to be added for each. Also, if an additional fill line is later added, the capacity of the ventilation system needs to be increased accordingly.

Safety factor. A 20 percent safety factor is generally used to account for minor seal leaks and hose leaks, dead spots, and occasional container ruptures.

The following is an example of the formula's use:

Assumptions: Under-the-cup filler, 3 cc release per container. A second machine in the propellant charging room is an indexing through-the-valve filler that fills each container three times at three separate stations with a loss per fill of 1 cc times 3 fills per container, which equals 3 cc released per container. Each machine is operating at 150 containers per minute. Propellant is isobutane; LEL is 1.8 percent (30.59 ft³/gal). Safety factor for leakage is 20 percent. LEL design level is 10 percent.

$$\text{Gal released per min} = \frac{(3.0 \text{ cc/container})(2)(150)(1.2)}{(3785.4 \text{ cc/gal})}$$

$$= 0.2853 \text{ gal/min}$$

$$\text{Required ft}^3/\text{min} = \frac{(100-1.8)(30.59 \text{ ft}^3/\text{gal})(0.2853 \text{ gal/min})}{(0.10)(1.8)}$$

$$= 4761 \text{ ft}^3/\text{min}$$

The equations assume that the released propellant gas and the entering make-up air will quickly mix and the resulting homogeneous mixture will then be exhausted. This is not the case. Thus, the calculations give results that will be on the conservative side in some locations within the propellant charging room and on the improvident side in others. For example, air entering the exhaust registers at points remote from the propellant filler will have a concentration of propellant that is much less than the average value upon which the ventilation system is designed.

Because some of the propellant will be swept into the nearest part of the exhaust system before being fully diluted, the apparent efficiency of the ventilating system is improved, providing an additional safety factor. This efficiency can be measured using combinations of velocity meters, explosimeters, and gas density plots. For all but a few percent of the volume in the typical propellant charging room, the concentration of propellant will be substantially less than the designed-for 10 percent of the LEL. This means that the gas detection heads might give very different readings if their positions are changed. Care needs to be exercised in determining the optimum location of the detector heads, especially if there are multiple propellant fillers in the room. In such cases, the use of three or four detection heads could be considered, rather than the two that are normally used.

A.5.4.2(F) See NFPA 91, *Standard for Exhaust Systems for Air Conveying of Vapors, Gases, Mists, and Noncombustible Particulate Solids*, for further information.

A.5.4.4 The enclosure required for the test bath provides protection for personnel and improves the efficiency of the local exhaust ventilation.

A.5.5.2 See also NFPA 497, *Recommended Practice for the Classification of Flammable Liquids, Gases, or Vapors and of Hazardous (Classified) Locations for Electrical Installations in Chemical Process Areas*.

A.5.6 See NFPA 77, *Recommended Practice on Static Electricity*, for further information.

A.5.7 The gas detection system should be provided with detection heads located inside the charging and pump rooms and just inside the conveyor openings into the charging or pump room and into the main production building. Detection heads should also be located within any conveyor enclosure between the charging or pump room and the main production building. Where flammable propellants are stored in a tank farm, the tank farm should be provided with an approved gas detection system and the signal sent to a constantly monitored location.

A.5.8.1 Dry-pipe or preaction systems are not allowed. Tests have shown that control of a fire involving aerosol products requires immediate application of water when the first sprinkler operates. Fire growth is rapid and, once thoroughly established, cannot be controlled by conventional or ESFR systems.

Any significant delay in sprinkler discharge will allow the fire to overtax the system. Increasing the design area for a dry-pipe or preaction system is not feasible because the delay will allow too many sprinklers to operate, thus overtaxing any practically designed water supply.

Paragraph 5.8.1 should not be interpreted as discouraging the use of a foam-water sprinkler system. As long as the ceiling density is not reduced, the use of a foam-water system does not introduce any known negative effects and could offer some additional benefits in combatting any spill fire that might result.

A.5.10.1 See Annex A of NFPA 15, *Standard for Water Spray Fixed Systems for Fire Protection*, for further information. Also, see NFPA 30, *Flammable and Combustible Liquids Code*.

A.5.13.3.1.1 This can be accomplished by the installation of a high pressure shutdown switch, or a safety relief valve installed in the propellant bypass return line [set at a minimum gauge pressure of 345 kPa (50 psi) below the setting of the hydrostatic relief valves], and vented into a vent pipe equipped with a flow switch or sensor.

A.5.13.3.3.1 This can be accomplished by the installation of a high pressure shutdown switch, or a safety relief valve installed in the propellant bypass return line (set at a minimum gauge pressure of 345 kPa (50 psi) below the setting of the hydrostatic relief valves), and vented into a vent pipe equipped with a flow switch or sensor.

A.5.14 The principal concern in the event of a shrink-wrap tunnel failure is the risk of aerosol container failure and subsequent fire. In the event of a container failure, significant ejection speeds, sympathetic failures of adjacent containers, and hot surfaces present serious potential exposures. In turn, ignition of flammable solvent or propellant vapor can result. The consequence of this is that an explosion can further augment the original ejection force. This can be a significant hazard to operators in the vicinity. Newly installed shrink-wrapping machines should be equipped with numerous safety features. Equipment suppliers should be advised of these features prior to placing orders.

The high fire risk associated with shrink-wrap tunnels should be considered when determining their location. Shrink-wrap acts as a very good insulator, which can facilitate overheating during its passage through the tunnel. Some containers can act as very efficient heat sinks resulting in fast heating of the containers if the film fails. This can also be exacerbated by the use of high proportions of substances with low specific heats in the formulations.

Automatic film failure detection, which switches off the heater and stops the machine in-feed, is necessary. The following is further guidance:

(1) The shrink-wrap machine design should ensure that containers are prevented from being trapped in the heating tunnel by internal obstructions.
(2) An alarm should be activated in the event of unplanned stoppage.
(3) The shrink-wrap machine should have a secondary means of keeping the tunnel conveyer moving in the event of power failure.
(4) In the event of conveyor power failure, standby power is recommended in place of a back-up air motor. This cuts in to energize the conveyor if any phase drops more than 10 percent. The in-feed gate and heaters should also automatically switch off and the operator should be alerted by a suitable alarm. If an air motor system is installed, a dedicated air receiver should be connected via metal

pipework. This receiver should store enough air to evacuate any "packs" in the tunnel and be constantly fed by the compressor via a non-return valve. An air pressure switch should be installed to interlock with the shrink-wrapper control system. Neither of these back-up systems will be of any use if the belt itself or transmission is broken, so a motion detector should also be installed to confirm belt movement and initiate the above shutdown if the belt stops during production.

(5) Operator protection training should include the use of appropriate personal protective equipment (PPE) in the event containers or collations must be removed manually during a breakdown or unplanned stoppage.

(6) Automatically operated fire suppression systems shall be installed in accordance with applicable NFPA codes and standards. Portable fire extinguishers should be provided and located in accordance with NFPA 10, *Standard for Portable Fire Extinguishers.*

(7) There should be a half-hour fire-resistant partition or other equivalent means to prevent the spread of fire between the shrink-wrapping machine and the remainder of the aerosol filling line.

(8) Access to and escape routes from the shrink-wrapping machine should be kept clear at all times.

(9) Supplies of packaging materials should be stored or staged in defined areas away from the shrink-wrapping machine.

(10) There should be an automatic device to detect film failure and prevent new collations from being allowed to enter the heating tunnel in the event of a film failure.

(11) A pusher rod with a flat plate on the end, specifically designed for the shape of the heating tunnel or equivalent system, should be provided. This will allow operators to rapidly clear the heating tunnel of all collations and containers in the event of a total conveyer failure.

(12) A suitable means of ensuring that trapped aerosol containers can be rapidly removed from the tunnel (because either the conveyor has stopped or they have caught on some obstruction) is essential. The inside of the tunnel should be designed with sloping sides to prevent loose containers from being retained under the heaters. The design of such a system needs to provide for the protection of operators removing containers trapped in the heating tunnel, as a fully pressurized aerosol container that fails — as well as its contents — can be ejected with considerable force. Therefore, a remote-operated or automatic mechanism or system could be preferable. The above procedure should only be carried out if aerosol containers have remained in the tunnel for a short time and the operator is aware that it is within a safe period.

(13) The operator should be provided with the necessary PPE and be trained in its proper use, the proper use of the pusher rod, and the risks involved.

(14) A switch should be installed to allow the power supply to the tunnel heat to be turned off in the event of an emergency.

(15) The tunnel heater power switch should be provided with automatic shutdown systems that are manually reset.

(16) An emergency air blower or other means of rapidly cooling the tunnel should be installed according to the specification provided by the equipment supplier, unless an automatic fire suppression system is provided.

(17) Detectors should be installed to count collations in and out of the heating tunnel to activate heater power cutouts and alarms and to stop in-feed gates in the event of a tunnel blockage.

(18) Heated surfaces can ignite burst containers, so attention must be provided to ensure container stability, especially when wrapping without trays. If there is a likelihood of unstable containers in this area, appropriate sensors should be installed to inhibit the in-feed gate until the containers are removed. Installing gaseous or dry chemical automatic protection into the shrink-wrapper tunnel is an effective way to directly reach the source of fire. Such systems can be activated by the operator from a safe location, or installed to automatically activate by optical flame detectors located at each end of the tunnel. In addition to the tunnel, the discharge nozzles should also cover the film sealing area.

(19) The fire suppression system should be connected to the building fire alarm system.

(20) Where conveyers feed shrink-wrapped collations to further automatic equipment downstream from the shrink-wrapping machine, there should be an out-feed light curtain or similar device to detect back-up from the downstream equipment and to stop the in-feed gate until there is no longer a backup.

(21) There should be a device installed to detect excess temperatures in the heating tunnel, producing an alarm, cutting power to the heaters, starting the air blowers (if installed), and stopping the in-feed gate.

(22) The excess temperature detector should be calibrated at regular specified intervals and the results recorded.

(23) A tunnel temperature indicator should be installed for operator information and maintenance purposes showing low, normal, and high/excess bands.

(24) The temperature indicator should be calibrated at regular specified intervals and the results recorded.

(25) All electrical resets on shrink-wrappers should be manually operated only.

(26) Safeguarding should be provided to prevent injury to operators from ejecting containers and contact with hot surfaces.

A.6.1.3 At the present time there have been no fire-retardant packaging systems tested that have demonstrated substantial mitigation of the fire hazards presented by aerosol products.

A.6.2 Fire tests and fire experience show that Level 1 aerosol products present relatively the same fire hazards as Class III commodities, as these are defined and described in NFPA 13, *Standard for the Installation of Sprinkler Systems.* In some cases, the AHJ or applicable fire or building regulations might require storage of such materials to be protected from fire. If fire protection is by means of automatic sprinklers, then the requirements of NFPA 13 should be used as a design basis.

A.6.3.2.2 Fire testing has not been performed on encapsulated pallets of cartoned aerosol products; however, this type of protection should be appropriate for this condition, based on testing of uncartoned aerosol products.

A.6.3.2.9 ESFR ceiling sprinklers are permitted to be used in conjunction with the in-rack sprinkler protection criteria in Table 6.3.2.7(e) through Table 6.3.2.7(l) where the following conditions are met:

(1) Roof height does not exceed 9.14 m (30 ft).
(2) Storage height does not exceed 7.62 m (25 ft).
(3) Clearance between top of storage and sprinkler deflectors is at least 0.91 m (3 ft).
(4) Ceiling sprinkler design criterion is 12 sprinklers operating at a gauge pressure of 517 kPa (75 psi).
(5) All in-rack sprinklers are quick-response type.

A.6.3.8.2.3.2 The 2.9 mm (9 gauge) chain-link fencing referred to by this paragraph refers to the standard industrial-grade chain link, such as is used for property fencing. Lighter-gauge fencing will not restrain rocketing aerosol containers, based on test experience.

A.6.3.9.1 See NFPA 80A, *Recommended Practice for Protection of Buildings from Exterior Fire Exposures*, for recommended separation.

A.8.3.3 See NFPA 51B, *Standard for Fire Prevention During Welding, Cutting, and Other Hot Work*, for further information.

A.8.7 See NFPA 77, *Recommended Practice on Static Electricity*, for further information.

Annex B   Mechanism of Fire Growth in Aerosol Containers

This annex is not a part of the requirements of this NFPA document but is included for informational purposes only.

B.1 Introduction. The automatic fire protection alternatives given in Chapter 6 of this code are derived from more than a dozen aerosol product fire tests conducted by a major insurance company in the late 1970s and early 1980s *[see Table B.1(a) and Table B.1(b)]*, and more than 50 small-, medium-, and large-scale tests sponsored by the aerosol products industry in the 1980s *[see Table B.1(c) through Table B.1(g)]*. This aerosol fire research represents a significant body of knowledge regarding aerosol fire development and control for various types of aerosol products in various storage and protection scenarios.

A complete and detailed history of these aerosol storage research efforts can be obtained on request from the Chemical Specialities Manufacturers Association, Inc., in the form of a series of articles entitled "An Industry Responds: A Technical History of the CSMA Aerosol Warehouse Storage Fire Protection Research Program." Send requests to the attention of the Director of Scientific Affairs, Chemical Specialities Manufacturers Association, Inc., 1913 I Street N.W., Washington, DC 20006.

Aerosol warehouse storage fires, using standard fire test igniters, begin as cardboard fires. The fire grows up the flue, burning off the aerosol carton faces, and there is usually a flame 1.5 m to 3.0 m (5 ft to 10 ft) above the top of the array before the first aerosol can ruptures and aerosols become involved in the fire. Depending on the type of aerosol, the first can rupture tends to occur at 30 seconds to 60 seconds after ignition in rack storage arrays and 90 seconds to 120 seconds in palletized storage arrays.

When aerosol containers begin to rupture, some of the heat from the fuel added by the aerosol goes quickly to the ceiling, while some is absorbed into other aerosol containers, bringing them closer to, or exceeding, their burst pressure. Early application of adequate densities of sprinkler water is the most effective way to control or suppress an aerosol fire, avoiding a chain reaction that can lead to loss of control. For this reason, ESFR protection is especially effective for aerosol products.

Table B.1(a)   Spray Sprinkler Tests

	Test No. 1	2	3	4	5	6	7
Type of Aerosol Base Product	Alcohol	Alcohol	Toluene	Alcohol	Toluene	Alcohol	Toluene
No. of Pallet Loads	8	24	8	12	12	8	1
Storage Configuration	Rack	Rack	Rack	Palletized	Palletized	2 × 2 × 2	Palletized
No. of Ceiling Sprinklers Operated	13	16	43	4	92	64	36
Time of Operation of First Sprinkler in min:sec	1:52	2:06	2:19	3:05	3:03	1:26	9:23
No. of In-Rack Sprinklers Operated	5	6	5	—	—	—	—
Maximum Near-Ceiling Gas Temperature in °F (°C)	1292 (700)	1334 (723)	1493 (812)	938 (503)	2216 (1213)	1789 (976)	1905 (1040)
Time of Maximum Gas Temperature in min:sec	3:19	5:41	3:48	3:09	4:54	4:26	9:58
Time Above 1000°F (538°C)	—	—	—	—	2:16	3:32	0:52
Maximum Near-Ceiling Steel Temperature in °F (°C)	642 (339)	815 (435)	973 (503)	378 (192)	1439 (782)	—	626 (330)
Aisle Jump	No	No	Yes	No	Yes	—	—
Fire Controlled	Yes	Yes	No	Yes	No	No	No

	All Tests
Test Location	Factory Mutual Test Center, West Glocester, Rhode Island; 30 ft (9 m) high test site.
Ignition	Two cellucotton rolls — 3 in. dia. × 3 in. long (7.5 cm × 7.5 cm), each soaked in 4 oz (118 ml) of gasoline.
Protection/Ceiling	½ in. (12.7 mm) standard orifice, 286°F (141°C) [165°F (74°C) in Test No. 6]; 10 ft × 10 ft (2.5 m × 2.5 m) spacing; approx. 0.30 gpm/ft² (12.2 L/min·m²) density.
Protection/In-Rack	Three ½ in. (12.7 mm) standard orifice, 165°F (74°C) rated, upright sprinklers at the first, second, and third tier levels; 30 psi (207 kPa) discharge pressure.

Table B.1(b) Spray Sprinkler Tests

	Test No.									
	1	2	3	4	5	6	7	8	9	10
Ceiling Sprinkler Density in gpm/ft² (L/min·m²)	0.6 (24)	0.6 (24)	0.6 (24)	0.3 (12)	0.6 (24)	0.3 (12)	0.3 (12)	0.3 (12)	0.6 (24)	0.3 (12)
Type of Aerosol Base Product	Toluene	Toluene	Toluene	Toluene	Paint	Alcohol	Perfume	Deodorant	Toluene	Butane
No. of Pallets	8	12	24	24	10	1	1	1	24	1
Storage Configuration (r = rack, p = palletized, 3 × 4 × 1 high)	r	p	r	r	p	—	—	—	p (2 high)	—
No. of Ceiling Sprinklers Operated	12	4	5	5	18	4	0	3	44	—
Time of Operation of First Sprinkler in min:sec	1:37	2:33	3:37	2:15	2:35	4:21	—	4:13	2:07	—
No. of In-Rack Sprinklers Operated	6	—	5	1	—	—	—	—	—	—
Maximum Near-Ceiling Gas Temperature in °F (°C)	1527 (830)	1177 (636)	790 (421)	1410 (765)	1343 (728)	697 (369)	165 (74)	520 (271)	2162 (189)	372 (1183)
Time of Maximum Gas Temperature in min:sec	3:32	2:34	3:32	2:17	4:02	4:27	4:50	3:57	4:03	6:13
Time Above 1000°F (538°C)	2:28	0:04	0:28	0:44	0:06	—	—	—	4:56	—
Maximum Near-Ceiling Steel Temperature in °F (°C)	835 (446)	417 (214)	213 (101)	375 (191)	323 (162)	170 (77)	100 (38)	177 (80)	1557 (117)	243 (847)
Aisle Jump	Yes	No	Yes	No	Yes	—	—	—	Yes	—
Fire Controlled	Yes	Yes	Yes	Yes	Yes	Yes	Yes	Yes	No	Yes

	All Tests
Test Location	Factory Mutual Test Center, West Glocester, Rhode Island; 30 ft (9 m) high test site.
Ignition	Two cellucotton rolls — 3 in. diam × 3 in. long (7.5 cm × 7.5 cm) each soaked in 4 oz (118 ml) of gasoline.
Protection/Ceiling	17/32 in. (13.5 mm) large orifice, 286°F (141°C); 10 ft × 10 ft (2.5 m × 2.5 m) spacing [Tests 1–3, 5, and 9]. ½ in. (12.7 mm) standard orifice, 286°F (141°C); 10 ft × 10 ft (2.5 m × 2.5 m) spacing [Tests 4, 6–8, and 10].
Protection/In-Rack	Three ½ in. (12.7 mm) orifice, 165°F (74°C) rated, upright sprinklers per tier; 30 psi (207 kPa) discharge pressure.

Table B.1(c) Tests on Product and Packaging Changes Data Summary Series 1

	Test No.					
	1	2	3	4	5	6
Type of Aerosol Base Product	Paint	Paint	Paint	Paint	Paint	Paint
Packaging Variable	—	Rim-vent-release cans	Fire retardant cartons	Shrink-wrapped pallets	Methylene chloride solvent	Metal overcaps
Test Results						
Sprinklers Operated	4	33	4	30	28	5
Maximum Ceiling Temperature in °F	1010	2141	980	1525	1881	1220
Time of First Can Rupture	1:31	1:20	1:56	1:25	1:18	1:36
1st Sprinkler Activation	2:15	1:40	2:40	2:13	1:45	1:55
Final Sprinkler Activation	2:22	5:09	4:12	5:22	4:55	3:06
Est. Product Damage	60%	70%	40%	80%	70%	75%
Comments	Fire controlled by four sprinklers in 9–10 min	Fire built rapidly out of control, reaching maximum intensity at 6 min	Fire controlled by four sprinklers in 6 min, after slow fire development	Increased fire intensity after 4 min required test to be aborted at 5:20	Increased fire intensity after 3 min required test to be aborted at 4:30	Fire controlled by five sprinklers in 9–10 min

All Tests

Test Location	20 ft ceiling (tests conducted on 40 ft × 40 ft metal platform).
Ignition	2-pallet array spaced 1 ft apart with ignition between pallets by two half-igniters (plastic bags containing 4 oz heptane on cotton rolls).
Protection	Standard orifice sprinklers with 286°F (141°C) links installed 10 ft apart; 29 psi constant water pressure delivering 0.3 gpm/ft^2.

For SI units, 1 ft = 0.3048 m; 1 ft^2 = 0.0929 m^2; 1 gpm/ft^2 = 40.743 L/min· m^2; 1 psi = 6.895 kPa; 1 gpm = 3.785 L/min.

Table B.1(d) Intermediate-Scale Tests Data Summary Series 2

	Test No.					
	1	2	3	4	5	6
Type of Aerosol Base Product	Hair spray	Hair spray	Air freshener	Furniture polish	Laundry pre-wash	Toluene/A-70
Pallet Configuration	2 × 2 × 2	2 × 2 × 3	1 × 2 × 1	1 × 2 × 1	1 × 2 × 1	1 × 2 × 1
Sprinkler	½ in.	17/32 in.	½ in.	½ in.	½ in.	½ in.
Link Temperature in °F	160	160	280	280	280	280
Water Pressure in psi	30	30	30	30	30	30
Water Density in gpm/ft^2	0.3	0.43	0.3	0.3	0.3	0.3
Test Results						
Sprinklers Operated	33	23	1	3	3	16
Maximum Ceiling Temperature in °F	1761	1475	659	603	653	1855
Time of First Can Rupture	1:48	1:50	1:45	1:54	1:51	1:50
1st Sprinkler Activation	2:02	2:05	3:05	6:08	4:17	2:16
Final Sprinkler Activation	6:36	4:50	—	6:10	4:20	4:48
Est. Product Damage	50%	75%	20%	50%	75%	65%
Comments	Poor control; intense fire for 15 min	Intensity of fire required test to be aborted at 8:20	Fire easily controlled in 5 min by single sprinkler	Fire controlled in 9 min after slow fire build-up	Fire reasonably well controlled in 10–12 min	Intense fire for 8–10 min before any control established

All Tests

Test Location	20 ft ceiling (tests conducted on 40 ft × 40 ft metal platform).
Ignition	Ignition by two half-igniters (plastic bags containing 4 oz heptane on cotton rolls).
Protection	Sprinklers installed on 10 ft grid.

For SI units, 1 ft = 0.3048 m; 1 ft^2 = 0.0929 m^2; 1 gpm/ft^2 = 40.743 L/min· m^2; 1 psi = 6.895 kPa; 1 gpm = 3.785 L/min.

Table B.1(e) Large-Drop Sprinkler Tests — Intermediate-Scale Data Summary Series 3

	_____ Test No. _____						
	1	2	3	4	5	6	7
Type of Aerosol Base Product	Hair spray	Hair spray	Hair spray	Paint	Furniture polish	Paint	Paint (RVR/MeCl)*
Pallet Configuration	2 × 2 × 3	2 × 2 × 3	2 × 2 × 3	2 × 2 × 3	2 × 2 × 3	2 × 2 × 2	1 × 2 × 1
Sprinklers	17/32 in.	0.64 in.	0.64 in.	0.64 in.	0.64 in.	0.64 in.	½ in.
Link Temperature in °F	160	160	160	160	160	160	280
Water Pressure in psi	56	50	25	75	50	75	30
Water Density in gpm/ft²	0.6	0.8	0.56	0.96	0.8	0.96	0.3
Test Results							
Sprinklers Operated	4	4	18	4	4	4	36
Maximum Ceiling Temperature in °F	1080	1645	1439	1350	1068	1111	2163
Time of First Can Rupture	1:48	1:45	1:46	1:35	1:56	1:47	1:20
1st Sprinkler Activation	1:56	1:54	1:53	1:43	2:27	2:01	1:47
Final Sprinkler Activation	2:00	2:01	4:52	1:47	2:28	2:08	3:24
Est. Product Damage	20%	20%	50%	40%	20%	20%	90%
Comments	Fire controlled in 6–8 min and suppressed by 15 min	Fire fully suppressed in 10 min	Inadequate control led to 18 sprinkler activations; potential for fire spread	Fire marginally controlled, but potential for fire spread	Fire controlled in 5–7 min	Fire well controlled in 4–5 min	Very intense fire; test aborted at 3:20

	All Tests
Test Location	20 ft ceiling (tests conducted on 40 ft × 40 ft metal platform).
Ignition	Ignition by two half-igniters (plastic bags containing 4 oz heptane on cotton rolls).
Protection	Sprinklers installed on 10 ft grid.

For SI units, 1 ft = 0.3048 m; 1 ft² = 0.0929 m²; 1 gpm/ft² = 40.743 L/min · m²; 1 psi = 6.895 kPa; 1 gpm = 3.785 L/min; 160°F = 71°C; 280°F = 138°C.
*Rim-vent release container; methylene chloride solvent.

Table B.1(f) Large-Drop Sprinkler Tests — Large-Scale and Intermediate-Scale Data Summary Series 4

	_____ Test No. _____				
	1	2	3	4	5
Type of Aerosol Base Product	Paint	Hair spray	Laundry pre-wash	Antiperspirant	Paint
Pallet Configuration	2-High	3-High	2 × 2 × 2	2 × 2 × 3	2 × 2 × 3
Sprinkler	0.64	0.64	0.64	0.64	0.64
Link Temperature in °F	160	160	160	160	160 (150 RTI)*
Water Pressure in psi	75	50	50	75	75
Water Density in gpm/ft²	0.96	0.8	0.8	0.96	0.96
Test Results					
Sprinklers Operated	4	7	4	7	4
Maximum Ceiling Temperature in °F	1158	1337	1116	1520	895
Time of First Can Rupture	1:30	1:33	2:24	1:45	1:34
1st Sprinkler Activation	1:49	1:44	2:52	1:49	1:43
Final Sprinkler Activation	1:52	3:42	3:09	6:43	1:48
Est. Product Damage	—	—	15%	50%	25%
Comments	Fire well controlled in 3–4 min; suppressed in 15–20 min. No fire spread.	Fire well controlled in 6–7 min, despite 2 sprinkler malfunctions. No fire spread.	Fire well controlled in 5 min; suppressed within 10–15 min. Fire spread unlikely.	Moderate control, fire persisted 25 min; probability for fire spread.	Fire well controlled in 5 min; suppressed in 15–20 min. Fire spread unlikely.

	All Tests
Test Location	25 ft ceiling (tests conducted on 40 ft × 40 ft metal platform).
Ignition	Ignition by two half-igniters (plastic bags containing 4 oz heptane on cotton rolls).
Protection	Sprinklers installed on 10 ft grid.

For SI units, 1 ft = 0.3048 m; 1 ft² = 0.0929 m²; 1 gpm/ft² = 40.743 L/min · m²; 1 psi = 6.895 kPa; 1 gpm = 3.785 L/min; 160°F = 71°C; 280°F = 138°C.
*Response Time Index of 150.

Table B.1(g) ESFR Tests

	\multicolumn{9}{c}{Test No.}
	1	2	3	4	5	6	7	8	9
Aerosol Base Product	Hair spray	Paint	Paint	Paint	Paint	Paint	Hair spray	Hair spray	Paint
Aerosol Product Classification	Level 2	Level 3	Level 3	Level 3	Level 3	Level 3	Level 2	Level 2	Level 3
Array Stack Height	Rack, 18 ft 10 in. (5.7 m)	Rack, 13 ft 10 in. (4.2 m)	Palletized, 15 ft 6 in. (4.7 m)	Rack, 13 ft 7 in. (4.1 m)	Rack, 13 ft 10 in. (4.2 m)	Rack, 13 ft 10 in. (4.2 m)	Rack, 13 ft 10 in. (4.2 m)	Rack, 18 ft 10 in. (5.7 m)	Rack, 13 ft 10 in. (4.2 m)
Ceiling clearance	6 ft 2 in. (1.9 m)	11 ft 2 in. (3.4 m)	9 ft 6 in. (2.9 m)	4 ft 2 in. (1.3 m)	11 ft 2 in. (3.4 m)	15 ft 0 in. (4.5 m)	15 ft 0 in. (4.5 m)	10 ft 0 in. (3 m)	15 ft 0 in. (4.5 m)
No. of Sprinklers above Ignition Point	4	4	4	2	1	1	1	2	1
Time of First Sprinkler Operation in min:sec	1:02	0:42	0:49	0:55	0:35	0:36	0:34	0:56	1:15
Time of Last Sprinkler Operation in min:sec	1:11	1:06	1:36	6:33	0:35	2:06	0:34	3:44	—
Total Sprinklers Operated	4	4	4	5	1	61	1	14	1
Peak Temperature in °F (°C)	1045 (563)	565 (296)	713 (378)	1421 (772)	256 (124)	1447 (786)	223 (106)	995 (535)	200 (93)
Time of First Container Rupture	1:03	1:01	1:29	0:52	None	0:44	0:46	1:01	0:10

Test Location Tests 1 through 5	25 ft ceiling (tests conducted on 40 ft × 40 ft metal platform).
Tests 6 through 9	30 ft ceiling.
Ignition Tests 1, 2, and 4 through 9	Ignition by four half-igniters (plastic bags containing 4 oz heptane on cotton rolls).
Test 3	Ignition by two half-igniters (plastic bags containing 4 oz heptane on cotton rolls).
Protection	Sprinklers installed on 10 ft grid.

Note: All of the above tests, except for Test 9, were conducted with 50 psi (3.45 bar) operating pressure. Test 9 used 75 psi (5.2 bar).

B.2 Rack Storage Arrays. The rack storage configuration is ideal for promoting fire development. The fuel is supported so that air has access to the fire from all sides and so that the stored commodity does not topple over, as it would in solid pile storage. A rack also has many areas that are shielded from ceiling sprinkler discharge.

Fire tests of rack storage configurations show a very consistent development pattern: the fire starts at a point and widens as it moves up the storage array, like a "V." When the fire reaches the second tier of storage, the flames fan out along the bottom of the pallet above and spread laterally to the face of the rack. Fireballs from rupturing aerosol cans, which usually measure 3 m (10 ft) in diameter, also spread fire to the face of the rack. Once the fire is established on the face of the rack, the fire spreads rapidly upward and outward horizontally in the classic "V" pattern, thus exposing more of the commodity. The fire on the face of the rack and within the transverse flue spaces of the rack structure also causes more aerosol containers to rupture. As additional containers rupture, uninvolved containers on the interior of the pallet load are now exposed to the fire.

Fire can jump the aisle space between two rows of racks in several ways. If the fire is severe enough, the radiant energy alone can be sufficient to ignite combustible cartons or commodities in the exposed rack. Fireballs from rupturing aerosol cans are large enough to engulf adjacent racks with flame. Occasionally, burning flammable liquid might be ejected from rupturing containers with enough force to reach the exposed storage.

In-rack sprinklers, located in the longitudinal flue space, are highly effective in preventing the fire from crossing into the other half of a double-row rack. Even in fire tests that were failures (i.e., the fire jumped the aisle to involve the target array), these in-rack sprinklers were successful in stopping the fire at the flue space. Cartons were burned, but no aerosol containers ruptured.

In-rack sprinklers located at the face of the rack structure have been shown to stop the spread of fire up the face of the rack. Their position within the rack structure allows them to wet down the face of the storage array that fronts on the aisle. This reduces the demand on the ceiling sprinkler system, which allows a reduction in the design density of the ceiling sprinkler system. Also, the ESFR sprinkler head operates fast enough and discharges water at a high enough density that it is capable of preventing fire spread up the face of the rack.

The combination of ESFR ceiling sprinklers and in-rack sprinklers was determined in this case to be acceptable based on the review of the original full-scale testing that was used to determine adequate protection using in-rack sprinklers and spray sprinklers at the ceiling. The low number of ceiling sprinklers that operated in the full-scale tests indicates that the substitution of ESFR sprinklers over racks with the same level of in-rack sprinkler protection would not result in a more severe fire. The in-rack sprinklers should be quick-response type and should meet the currently required installation rules provided in Table 6.3.2.7(e) through Table 6.3.2.7(l).

B.3 Palletized Storage Arrays. Palletized storage does not offer the same conducive conditions for fast fire growth as rack storage, but can result in persistent fires if sprinklers are not designed for proper protection.

Early aerosol fire tests showed that standard spray sprinkler protection had difficulty controlling Level 2 and Level 3 aerosol products stacked more than 1.5 m (5 ft) high under a 9 m (30 ft) ceiling. A major testing program sponsored by the aerosol industry was therefore begun to seek more cost-effective storage and protection alternatives.

The first series in that program investigated packaging and formulation alternatives in a series of small-scale tests on Level 3 aerosol paint products, protected by spray sprinklers [13 mm (½ in.) orifice] under a 6.1 m (20 ft) ceiling. The packaging variables were rim-vent release cans, shrink-wrap replacing cardboard cartons, metal instead of plastic overcaps, fire-resistant cardboard cartons, and methylene chloride replacing some of the petroleum distillate solvents.

None of these alternatives proved significantly beneficial as compared to the standard "control" aerosol product. The rim-vent release, shrink-wrap, and methylene chloride alternatives resulted in harder-to-control fires. The metal overcap product was essentially equivalent to the control. The fire-resistant cartons primarily resulted only in delaying the fire buildup, but had little benefit once aerosols were involved.

Further aerosol fire testing evaluated higher water densities and larger-orifice sprinkler heads to protect higher stacking in palletized storage arrays of Levels 1, 2, and 3 aerosol products under low-to-medium ceiling heights [6.1 m to 7.6 m (20 ft to 25 ft)]. Numerous successful protection alternatives were found. To properly protect each class of aerosol product stored in higher stack height and higher ceiling height scenarios was found to require higher water densities from larger-orifice [13 mm to 16 mm (17/32 in. to 0.64 in.)] sprinklers fitted with low-temperature fusible links.

The final improvement in aerosol fire protection was found by using an even faster response sprinkler. ESFR sprinklers, which are fitted with extremely fast-responding, low-temperature links [71°C (160°F), Response Time Index = 50], were found capable of protecting high-stack palletized aerosol product storage under ceilings up to 9 m (30 ft) high, as well as rack storage without in-rack sprinklers. In virtually all of the successful ESFR tests, the fire was not only controlled, but quickly suppressed and, in some cases, totally extinguished. The success of ESFR protection for aerosol product storage could be due primarily to the ability of these sprinklers to be activated by cardboard on fire and to begin to fight the fire before any aerosols are involved.

B.4 Data from Full-Scale Rack Storage Fire Tests of Various Aerosol Products in Metal Containers. Table B.4(a) through Table B.4(g) are taken from Tables A-1 through A-7 of the FM Global Research Technical Report written by Joan Troup, "Full-Scale Fire Tests: Sprinkler Protection for Rack Storage of Plastic-Wrapped (Uncartoned) Aerosols." These tables summarize a full-scale test series conducted by FM Global Research and sponsored by the Alternative Aerosol Packaging Fire Test Steering Committee. The testing investigated protection needs for uncartoned aerosol storage arrangements.

Table B.4(h) is taken from Table 1 of the FM Global Research Report, "Large-Scale Fire Test 1 on Aerosol Product Storage." This table summarizes a full-scale test conducted by FM Global Research of aerosol products containing a very high level of vegetable oil in 227 g (8 oz) steel cans/135 cartons per pallet load. The testing investigated protection needs for palletized aerosol storage arrangements.

Table B.4(i) is taken from Table 1 of the FM Global Research Report, "Large-Scale Fire Test 2 on Aerosol Product Storage." This table summarizes a full-scale test series conducted by FM Global Research of aerosol products containing a very high level of vegetable oil in 227 g (8 oz) steel cans/125 cartons per pallet load. The testing investigated protection needs for palletized aerosol storage arrangements.

Table B.4(a) Summary — Large-Scale Fire Test 1

Test Number & Date	Test 1	February 3, 1998
Test Site Ceiling Height (ft) [m]		30 [9.1]
Commodity or Type of Fuel		Generic Level 3 Aerosol*
Array Size & Storage Arrangement		Double-Row Rack
Storage Height (ft) [m]		14 [4.3]
Number of Storage Levels		3
Aisle Width (ft) [m]		4 [1.2]
Ignition Centered Below (Number of Sprinklers)		1
Sprinkler Type		Suppression
Sprinkler K-Factor (gpm/(psi)$^{1/2}$) [L/min/(kPa)$^{1/2}$]		14 [20]
Sprinkler Temperature Rating (°F) [°C]		165 [74]
Sprinkler Nominal Response Time Index (ft$^{1/2}$sec$^{1/2}$) [m$^{1/2}$sec$^{1/2}$]		50 [28]
Sprinkler Spacing (ft × ft) [m × m]		10 × 10 [3.05 × 3.05]
Sprinkler Discharge Pressure (psi) [bar]		75 [5.2]
Sprinkler Nominal Discharge (gpm) [L/min]		120 [454]
Fire Test Results		
First Sprinkler Operation (min:sec)		1:17
Last Sprinkler Operation (min:sec)		7:45
Total Sprinklers Opened		5
Peak Gas Temperature Over Ignition (°F) [°C]		191 [88]
Peak Steel Temperature Over Ignition (°F) [°C]		128 [53]
Peak Heat Flux (Btu/ft^2/sec) [kJ/m^2/sec]		5.0 [57]
Estimated Equivalent Number of Pallet Loads Damaged		3
Test Termination — Time After Ignition (min)		9:00‡

*Corrugated paper tray, 2 in. (51 mm) high, containing twelve 12 oz (360 ml) steel cans, encased in plastic film shrink wrapping.
‡Forced test termination due to growing fire.
Source: FM Global Research.

Table B.4(b) Summary — Large-Scale Fire Test 2

Test Number	Test 2 June 23, 1998
Building Test Site Ceiling Height (ft) [m]	30 [9.1]
Commodity or Type of Fuel	Generic Level 3 Aerosol*
Storage Arrangement	Double-Row Rack
Storage Height (ft) [m]	19 [5.8]
Number of Storage Levels	4
Aisle Width (ft) [m]	8 [2.4]
Ignition Centered Below (Number of Ceiling Sprinklers)	4

Ceiling Level Sprinkler Details

Sprinkler Temperature Rating (°F) [°C]	286 [141]
Sprinkler K-Factor (gpm/(psi)$^{1/2}$) [L/min/(kPa)$^{1/2}$]	8 [11.5]
Sprinkler Nominal Response Time Index (ft$^{1/2}$sec$^{1/2}$) [m$^{1/2}$sec$^{1/2}$]	240 [133]
Sprinkler Spacing (ft × ft) [m × m]	10 × 10 [3.05 × 3.05]
Sprinkler Discharge Pressure (psi) [bar]	56 [3.9]
Sprinkler Nominal Discharge (gpm) [L/min]	60 [227]

In-Rack Sprinkler Details (Three Levels)

Sprinkler Temperature Rating (°F) [°C]	165 [74]
Sprinkler K-Factor (gpm/(psi)$^{1/2}$) [L/min/(kPa)$^{1/2}$]	8 [11.5]
Sprinkler Nominal Response Time Index (ft$^{1/2}$sec$^{1/2}$) [m$^{1/2}$sec$^{1/2}$]	50 [28]
Longitudinal Flue Sprinkler On-line Spacing (ft) [m]	4 [1.2]
Face Sprinkler On-line Spacing (ft) [m]	8¼ [2.5]
Sprinkler Discharge Pressure (psi) [bar]	30 [2.1]

Fire Test Results

Longitudinal Flue In-Rack Sprinkler Operations (min:sec)	2:04, 2:05, 2:27
In-Rack Sprinkler Operations (min:sec)	16:56
Total Sprinklers Opened: In-Rack/Ceiling	4/None
Peak Gas Temperature Over Ignition (°F) [°C]	0.46 [5.2]
Peak Steel Temperature Over Ignition (°F) [°C]	210 [99]
Peak Heat Flux (Btu/ft^2/sec) [kJ/m^2/sec]	98 [37]
Estimated Equivalent Number of Pallet Loads Damaged	< 1½
Test Termination — Time After Ignition (min)	30‡

*Corrugated paper tray, 2 in. (51 mm) high, containing twelve 12 oz (360 ml) steel cans, encased in plastic film shrink wrapping; 85 tray-packs per pallet load.
‡Hose lines used to extinguish residual fires.
Source: FM Global Research.

Table B.4(c) Summary — Large-Scale Fire Test 3

Test Number & Date	Test 3 June 25, 1998
Building Test Site Ceiling Height (ft) [m]	30 [9.1]
Commodity or Type of Fuel	Level 2 Aerosol — Hair Spray*
Storage Arrangement	Double-Row Rack
Storage Height (ft) [m]	14 [4.3]
Number of Storage Levels	3
Aisle Width (ft) [m]	4 [1.2]
Ignition Centered Below (Number of Sprinklers)	1
Sprinkler Type	Suppression
Sprinkler K-Factor (gpm/(psi)$^{1/2}$) [L/min/(kPa)$^{1/2}$]	14 [20]
Sprinkler Temperature Rating (°F) [°C]	165 [74]
Sprinkler Nominal Response Time Index (ft$^{1/2}$sec$^{1/2}$) [m$^{1/2}$sec$^{1/2}$]	50 [28]
Sprinkler Spacing (ft × ft) [m × m]	10 × 10 [3.05 × 3.05]
Sprinkler Discharge Pressure (psi) [bar]	75 [5.2]
Sprinkler Nominal Discharge (gpm) [L/min]	120 [454]

Fire Test Results

First Sprinkler Operation (min:sec)	1:23
Last Sprinkler Operation (min:sec)	1:23
Total Sprinklers Opened	1
First/Last Audible Aerosol Rupture (min:sec)	0:41/1:40
Peak Gas Temperature Over Ignition (°F) [°C]	208 [98]
Peak Steel Temperature Over Ignition (°F) [°C]	88 [31]
Peak Heat Flux (Btu/ft^2/sec) [kJ/m^2/sec]	1.6 [18]
Estimated Equivalent Number of Pallet Loads Damaged	< 0.25
Test Termination — Time After Ignition (min)	6‡

*Paperboard tray, 1½ in. (38 mm) high, containing six 7 oz (200 ml) steel cans, encased in plastic film shrink wrapping; 268 tray-packs per pallet load.
‡Hose line used to extinguish small residual fire.
Source: FM Global Research.

Table B.4(d) Summary — Large-Scale Fire Test 4

Test Number & Date	Test 4 Jan. 29, 1999
Building Test Site Ceiling Height (ft) [m]	30 [9.1]
Commodity or Type of Fuel	Level 3 Aerosol — Paint[a]
Storage Arrangement	Double-Row Rack
Storage Height (ft) [m]	24 [7.3]
Number of Storage Levels	5
Aisle Width (ft) [m]	8 [2.4]
Ignition Centered Below (Number of Ceiling Sprinklers)	2[b]

continues

Table B.4(d) Continued

Test Number & Date	Test 4 Jan. 29, 1999
Ceiling Level Sprinkler Protection Details	
Sprinkler Type	Suppression
Sprinkler K-Factor (gpm/(psi)$^{1/2}$) [L/min/(kPa)$^{1/2}$]	14 [20]
Sprinkler Temperature Rating (°F) [°C]	165 [74]
Sprinkler Nominal Response Time Index (ft$^{1/2}$sec$^{1/2}$) [m$^{1/2}$sec$^{1/2}$]	50 [28]
Sprinkler Spacing (ft × ft) [m × m]	10 × 10 [3.05 × 3.05]
Sprinkler Discharge Pressure (psi) [bar]	50 [3.4]
Sprinkler Nominal Discharge (gpm) [L/min]	100 [388]
In-Rack Sprinkler Protection Details (Installed at First and Third Storage Levels)	
Sprinkler Nominal Response Time Index (ft$^{1/2}$sec$^{1/2}$) [m$^{1/2}$sec$^{1/2}$]	50 [28]
Sprinkler K-Factor (gpm/(psi)$^{1/2}$) [L/min/(kPa)$^{1/2}$]	8 [11.5]
Sprinkler Temperature Rating (°F) [°C]	165 [74]
Longitudinal Flue Sprinkler Spacing (ft, apart) [m, apart]	4 [1.2]
Sprinkler Discharge Pressure (psi) [bar]	30 [2.1]
Fire Test Results	
Total Sprinkler Operations: In-Rack/Ceiling	2/3
Longitudinal Flue Sprinkler Operations: 1st Tier and 3rd Tier (min:sec)	1:24, 1:07
Ceiling Sprinkler Operations (min:sec)	1:57, 1:58, 1:59
Peak Gas Temperature Over Ignition (°F) [°C]	394 [201]
Peak Steel Temperature Over Ignition (°F) [°C]	95 [35]
Peak Heat Flux (Btu/ft^2/sec) [kJ/m^2/sec]	1.4 [16]
Estimated Equivalent Number of Pallet Loads Damaged	< 1
Test Termination — Time After Ignition (min)	20[c]

[a]Corrugated paper tray, containing twelve 10 oz (300 ml) steel cans of paint, encased in plastic film shrink wrapping; 135 tray-packs per pallet load.
[b]Offset ignition.
[c]Hose used to extinguish small residual fires.
Source: FM Global Research.

Table B.4(e) Summary — Large-Scale Fire Test 5

Test Number & Date	Test 5 February 4, 1999
Test Site Ceiling Height (ft) [m]	30 [9.1]
Commodity or Type of Fuel	Level 3 Aerosol — Air Freshener[a]
Storage Arrangement	Double-Row Rack
Storage Height (ft) [m]	14 [4.3]
Number of Storage Levels	3
Aisle Width (ft) [m]	8 [2.4]
Ignition Centered Below (Number of Sprinklers)	1
Sprinkler Type	Suppression
Sprinkler K-Factor (gpm/(psi)$^{1/2}$) [L/min/(kPa)$^{1/2}$]	25.2 [36.3]
Sprinkler Temperature Rating (°F) [°C]	165 [74]
Sprinkler Nominal Response Time Index (ft$^{1/2}$sec$^{1/2}$) [m$^{1/2}$sec$^{1/2}$]	50 [28]
Sprinkler Spacing (ft × ft) [m × m]	10 × 10 [3.05 × 3.05]
Sprinkler Discharge Pressure (psi) [bar]	35 [2.4]
Sprinkler Nominal Discharge (gpm) [L/min]	150 [568]
Fire Test Results	
First Sprinkler Operation (min:sec)	0:49
Last Sprinkler Operation (min:sec)	5:14
Total Sprinklers Opened	9
Peak Gas Temperature Over Ignition (°F) [°C]	204 [96][b]
Peak Steel Temperature Over Ignition (°F) [°C]	137 [58]
Peak Heat Flux (Btu/ft^2/sec) [kJ/m^2/sec]	0.46 [5.2]
Estimated Equivalent Number of Pallet Loads Damaged	3
Test Termination — Time After Ignition (min)	10:00[c]

[a]Corrugated paper tray, 2 in. (51 mm) high, containing twelve 7 oz (200 ml) steel cans, encased in plastic film shrink wrapping.
[b]Highest temperature of 328°F (164°C) recorded 10 ft (3.05 m) east of ignition.
[c]Forced test termination due to growing fire.
Source: FM Global Research.

Table B.4(f) Summary — Large-Scale Fire Test 6

Test Number & Date	Test 6 June 2, 1999
Building Test Site Ceiling Height (ft) [m]	30 [9.1]
Commodity or Type of Fuel	Level 3 Aerosol — Air Freshener[a]
Storage Arrangement	Double-Row Rack
Storage Height (ft) [m]	24 [7.3]
Number of Storage Levels	5
Aisle Width (ft) [m]	8 [2.4]
Ignition Centered Below (Number of Ceiling Sprinklers)	2[b]

Table B.4(f) Continued

Test Number & Date	Test 6 June 2, 1999
Ceiling Level Sprinkler Protection Details	
Sprinkler Type	Suppression
Sprinkler K-Factor (gpm/(psi)$^{1/2}$) [L/min/(kPa)$^{1/2}$]	14 [20]
Sprinkler Temperature Rating (°F) [°C]	165 [74]
Sprinkler Nominal Response Time Index (ft$^{1/2}$sec$^{1/2}$) [m$^{1/2}$sec$^{1/2}$]	50 [28]
Sprinkler Spacing (ft × ft) [m × m]	10 × 10 [3.05 × 3.05]
Sprinkler Discharge Pressure (psi) [bar]	50 [3.4]
Sprinkler Nominal Discharge (gpm) [L/min]	100 [388]
In-Rack Sprinkler Protection Details *(Installed at First and Third Storage Levels)*	
Sprinkler K-Factor (gpm/(psi)$^{1/2}$) [L/min/(kPa)$^{1/2}$]	8 [11.5]
Sprinkler Temperature Rating (°F) [°C]	165 [74]
Sprinkler Nominal Response Time Index (ft$^{1/2}$sec$^{1/2}$) [m$^{1/2}$sec$^{1/2}$]	50 [28]
Longitudinal Flue Sprinkler Spacing (ft, apart) [m, apart]	4 [1.2]
Sprinkler Discharge Pressure (psi) [bar]	30 [2.1]
Fire Test Results	
Total Sprinkler Operations: In-Rack/Ceiling	2/6
Longitudinal Flue In-Rack Sprinkler Operations: First Tier and Third Tier (min:sec)	2:27, 1:59
First Ceiling Sprinkler Operation (min:sec)	1:48
Last Ceiling Sprinkler Operation (min:sec)	2:11
Peak Gas Temperature Over Ignition (°F) [°C]	326 [163]
Peak Steel Temperature Over Ignition (°F) [°C]	160 [71]
Peak Heat Flux (Btu/ft^2/sec) [kJ/m^2/sec]	1.04 [12]
Estimated Equivalent Number of Pallet Loads Damaged	8
Test Termination — Time After Ignition (min)	25[c]

[a]Corrugated paper tray, containing twelve 7 oz (200 ml) steel cans of air freshener, encased in plastic film shrink wrapping; 119 tray-packs per pallet load.
[b]Offset ignition.
[c]Hoses and monitor nozzles used to extinguish numerous shielded fires.
Source: FM Global Research.

Table B.4(g) Summary — Large-Scale Fire Test 7

Test Number & Date	Test 7 Sept 27, 1999
Building Test Site Ceiling Height (ft) [m]	30 [9.1]
Commodity or Type of Fuel	Level 3 Aerosol — Air Freshener[*]
Storage Arrangement	Double-Row Rack
Storage Height (ft) [m]	24 [7.3]
Number of Storage Levels	5
Aisle Width (ft) [m]	8 [2.4]
Ignition Centered Below (Number of Ceiling Sprinklers)	2
Ceiling Level Sprinkler Protection Details	
Sprinkler Type	Suppression
Sprinkler K-Factor (gpm/(psi)$^{1/2}$) [L/min/(kPa)$^{1/2}$]	14 [20]
Sprinkler Temperature Rating (°F) [°C]	165 [74]
Sprinkler Nominal Response Time Index (ft$^{1/2}$sec$^{1/2}$) [m$^{1/2}$sec$^{1/2}$]	50 [28]
Sprinkler Spacing (ft × ft) [m × m]	10 × 10 [3.05 × 3.05]
Sprinkler Discharge Pressure (psi) [bar]	50 [3.4]
Sprinkler Nominal Discharge (gpm) [L/min]	100 [388]
In-Rack Sprinkler Protection Details *(Installed at First, Second, Third and Fourth Storage Levels)*	
Sprinkler K-Factor (gpm/(psi)$^{1/2}$) [L/min/(kPa)$^{1/2}$]	8 [11.5]
Sprinkler Temperature Rating (°F) [°C]	165 [74]
Sprinkler Nominal Response Time Index (ft$^{1/2}$sec$^{1/2}$) [m$^{1/2}$sec$^{1/2}$]	50 [28]
Longitudinal Flue Sprinkler Spacing (ft, apart) [m, apart]	4 [1.2]
Sprinkler Discharge Pressure (psi) [bar]	30 [2.1]
Fire Test Results	
Total Sprinkler Operations: In-Rack/Ceiling	4/5
Longitudinal Flue In-Rack Sprinkler Operations: Third, First, Fourth and Second Tiers (min:sec)	1:51, 1:53, 1:55, 1:55
Ceiling Sprinkler Operations (min:sec)	1:44, 1:46, 1:58, 2:00, 2:01
Peak Gas Temperature Over Ignition (°F) [°C]	589 [309]
Peak Steel Temperature Over Ignition (°F) [°C]	141 [61]
Peak Heat Flux (Btu/ft^2/sec) [kJ/m^2/sec]	0.84 [9.5]
Estimated Equivalent Number of Pallet Loads Damaged	6
Test Termination — Time After Ignition (min)	25[‡]

[*]Corrugated paper tray, containing twelve 7 oz (200 ml) steel cans of air freshener, encased in plastic film shrink wrapping; 119 tray-packs per pallet load.
[‡]Hoses and monitor nozzles used to extinguish numerous shielded fires.
Source: FM Global Research.

Table B.4(h) Summary — Large-Scale Fire Test 1 on Aerosol Product Storage

Test Number & Date	Test 1	December 18, 2002
Building Test Site Ceiling Height (ft) [m]		30 [9.1]
Commodity or Type of Fuel		Aerosol Cooking Oil*
Array Size and Storage Arrangement		Large-Scale, Double-Row Rack
Storage Height (ft) [m]		14 [4.3]
Number of Storage Levels		3
Aisle Width (ft) [m]		8 [2.4]
Ignition Centered Below (Number of Sprinklers)		4
Sprinkler Type and Orifice Diameter (in.) [mm]		Standard Upright (½) [13]
Sprinkler Discharge Coefficient (K-Factor) (gpm/(psi)$^{1/2}$) [L/min/(kPa)$^{1/2}$]		5.6 [8.1]
Sprinkler Temperature Rating (°F) [°C]		286 [171]
Sprinkler Nominal Response Time Index (RTI) [(ft/s)$^{1/2}$] [(m/s)$^{1/2}$]		250 [138]
Sprinkler Spacing (ft × ft) [m × m]		10 × 10 [3.05 × 3.05]
Sprinkler Discharge Pressure (psi) [bar]		15.5 [1.07]
Sprinkler Nominal Discharge Density (gpm/ft^2) [mm/min]		0.22 [9]
Fire Test Results		
Total Sprinklers Opened		49*‡
First/Last Sprinkler Operation Times (min:s)		1:37 / 3:00‡
Peak Ceiling Level Gas Temperature (°F) [°C] and Time (min:s)		1717 [936]@3:00‡
Maximum One Minute Average Gas Temperature (°F) [°C]		1480 [804]‡
Peak Ceiling Level Steel Temperature (°F) [°C] and Time (min:s)		569 [298] @3:00‡
Maximum One Minute Average Steel Temperature (°F) [°C]		361 [183]‡
First audible sounds of cans venting/rupturing (min:s)		1:13 / 2:02
Test Termination — Time after ignition (min:s)		3:00‡

*Corrugated cartons containing twelve 227 g (8 oz) steel cans of aerosol vegetable oil; 135 cartons per pallet load.
‡Test required to be terminated early. Additional sprinkler operations, higher peak temperature values, and more extensive fire damage would have occurred.
Source: FM Global Research.

Table B.4(i) Summary — Large-Scale Fire Test 2 on Aerosol Product Storage

Test Number & Date	Test 2	February 12, 2003
Building Test Site Ceiling Height (ft) [m]		30 [9.1]
Commodity or Type of Fuel		Aerosol Cooking Oil*
Array Size and Storage Arrangement		Large-Scale, Double-Row Rack
Storage Height (ft) [m]		14 [4.3]
Number of Storage Levels		3
Aisle Width (ft) [m]		8 [2.4]
Ignition Centered Below (Number of Sprinklers)		4
Sprinkler Type and Orifice Diameter (in.) [mm]		ELO Upright (⅝) [16]
Sprinkler Discharge Coefficient (K-Factor) (gpm/(psi)$^{1/2}$) [L/min/(kPa)$^{1/2}$]		11.2 [16.2]
Sprinkler Temperature Rating (°F) [°C]		165 [74]
Sprinkler Nominal Response Time Index (RTI) ((ft-s)$^{1/2}$) [(m-s)$^{1/2}$]		250 [138]
Sprinkler Spacing (ft × ft) [m × m]		10 × 10 [3.05 × 3.05]
Sprinkler Discharge Pressure (psi) [bar]		29 [2.0]
Sprinkler Nominal Discharge Density (gpm/ft^2) [mm/min]		0.60 [24]
Fire Test Results		
Total Sprinklers Opened		22
First/Last Sprinkler Operation Times (min:s)		1:23 / 3:54‡
Peak Ceiling Level Gas Temperature (°F) [°C] and Time (min:s)		1355 [735]@4:07‡
Maximum One Minute Average Gas Temperature (°F) [°C]		1277 [692]‡
Peak Ceiling Level Steel Temperature (°F) [°C] and Time (min:s)		286 [141] @5:00‡
Maximum One Minute Average Steel Temperature (°F) [°C]		245 [118]‡
Cans noticeable venting / first audible sounds of cans rupturing (min:s)		1:08 / 2:04
Test Termination — Time after ignition (min:s)		5:00‡

*Corrugated cartons containing twelve 227 g (8 oz) steel cans of aerosol vegetable oil; 125 cartons per pallet load.
‡Test was terminated early. It is possible that additional sprinkler operations, higher peak temperature values, and more extensive fire damage would have occurred.
Source: FM Global Research.

B.5 Data from Various Palletized Aerosol Products in Plastic Containers Fire Tests. Beginning with the first edition of NFPA 30B in 1990, plastic aerosol containers have been limited to a maximum size of 118 ml (4 fl oz) while metal aerosol containers have had a maximum size of 1000 ml (33.8 fl oz). This is based on both the U.S. Department of Transportation (DOT) limitations and the absence of fire research with plastic aerosol containers. The DOT has recently removed the smaller size restriction on plastic aerosol containers. Plastic containers for combustible and flammable liquids have been found to be a greater fire risk than metal containers. The assumption is then that plastic might pose a greater risk than metal when used as containers for aerosol products. The recent removal of the DOT limitation has prompted the beginning of fire research with plastic aerosol containers. Initial tests are now recorded in Annex B.

Table B.5(a) is taken from Table 1 of the Underwriters Laboratories Inc. Research Technical Report, "Palletized Plastic Aerosol Storage Testing Result." This table summarizes a full-scale test conducted by Underwriters Laboratories and sponsored by a manufacturer of aerosol products. This test of aerosols in plastic containers on wood pallets was conducted with large drop sprinkler protection.

Table B.5(a) Large Drop Sprinkler Protection of Aerosol Products of Palletized Plastic Aerosol Storage Fire Testing

Test Number & Date	Test 1 9/29/2009
Test Parameters	
Storage Type	Palletized
Commodity Type	Aerosol in Plastic Containers
Commodity Description	Foam Shaving Cream, Log (No. 9114)
Main Test Array of Pallets	2 wide by 2 long by 3 high
Nominal Pallet Storage Height (ft)[m]	14 [4.3]
Building Test Site Ceiling Height (ft)[m]	25 [7.6]
Sprinkler to Commodity Clearance (ft)[m]	10 ft, 2 in. [3.1]
Ignition Location	Centered Between Four Sprinklers
Nominal Deflector to ceiling (in.)[mm]	7 [178]
Sprinkler Temperature Rating	155°F (Standard Response) [68°C]
Ceiling Sprinklers	Upright K-11.2 Large Drop
Sprinkler Spacing (branchline by sprinkler) (ft)[m]	10 × 10 [3.05 × 3.05]
Applied Flowing Pressure (psi)(bar)	50 [3.4]
Applied Sprinkler Density (gpm/ft²) [mm/min]	0.79 [32]
Fire Test Results	
Length of Test (min:sec)	32:00
Number of Operated Ceiling Sprinklers	4
Time of First Noticeable Container Rupture (min:sec)	0:55
Time of Flame Breach at Top of Array (min:sec)	0:59
First Ceiling Sprinkler Operation (min:sec)	1:23
Last Ceiling Sprinkler Operation (min:sec)	1:33
Peak Gas Temperature at Gas Above Ignition (°F)[C°]	1242 [672]
Maximum 1 Minute Average Steel Temperature Above Ignition (°F)[C°]	583 [306]
Peak Steel Temperature at Ceiling Above Ignition (°F)[C°]	165 [74]
Maximum 1 Minute Average Steel Temperature Above Ignition (°F)[C°]	146 [63]
Estimated Product Damage	5.2%

Table B.5(b) is taken from Table E-1 of the Underwriters Laboratories Inc. Research Technical Report, "Large Drop Sprinkler Protection of Palletized Storage of Aerosols in Plastic Containers on Wood Pallets Testing Result." This table summarizes a full-scale palletized array test conducted by Underwriters Laboratories and sponsored by a manufacturer of aerosol products. This test of aerosols in plastic containers on wood pallets was conducted with large drop sprinkler protection.

Table B.5(b) Large Drop Sprinkler Protection of Palletized Storage of Aerosols in Plastic Containers on Wood Pallets

Test Number & Date	Test 1 4/29/2008
Test Parameters	
Storage Type	Palletized
Commodity Type	Aerosol in Plastic Containers*
Main Test Array of Pallets	2 wide × 2 long × 3 high
Nominal Pallet Storage Height (ft)[m]	10 [3.05]
Ceiling Height (ft)[m]	30 [9.1]
Sprinkler to Commodity Clearance (ft)[m]	19 ft, 5 in. [5.9]
Ignition Location	Centered between four sprinklers
Nominal Deflector to Ceiling (in.)[mm]	7 [178]
Sprinkler Temperature Rating (°F)[°C]	155°F (Standard Response) [68°C]
Ceiling Sprinklers	Upright K-11.2 Large Drop
Sprinkler Spacing (branchline by sprinkler) (ft)[m]	10 × 10 [3.05 × 3.05]
Applied Flowing Pressure (psi)[bar]	75 [5.2]
Applied Sprinkler Density (gpm/ft²)[mm/min]	0.97 [39.5]
Fire Test Results	
Length of Test (min)	32
Number of Operating Sprinklers	4
Time of First Noticeable Container Rupture (min:sec)	1:12
Time of First Sprinkler Operation (min:sec)	1:47
Time of Last Sprinkler Operation (min:sec)	1:49
Peak Gas Temperature at Ceiling Above Ignition (°F)[C°]	884 [473]
Maximum 1 Minute Average Gas Temperature (°F)[C°]	472 [244]
Peak Steel Temperature at Ceiling Above Ignition (°F)[C°]	173 [78]
Maximum 1 Minute Average Steel Beam Temperature (°F)[C°]	168 [75]
Estimated Product Damage	50%

*Nominal 851 g (30 oz) plastic containers filled with a 35% ethanol/65% water mixture with propane, butane, and isobutane used as a propellant. The calculated heat of combustion was reported to be 10.85 kJ/g. UL did not verify the ingredients or the heat of combustion of this reported mixture. This information was provided by the test sponsor.

Source: Underwriters Laboratories Inc.

Annex C Determining the Classification Level of Aerosol Products in Metal Containers

This annex is not a part of the requirements of this NFPA document but is included for informational purposes only.

C.1 Section 1.7 provides formulation-based criteria for classifying aerosol products into three categories that require different levels of protection. These criteria are based on dozens of fire tests involving sprinklers and other relevant data on current aerosol product formulations. Because exact aerosol formulation data is often proprietary, it will be necessary for aerosol manufacturers to classify each aerosol product and communicate such information through carton marking as per Section 1.8 and 6.1.2. In addition, this communication can also be provided through other appropriate means such as material safety data sheets (MSDS).

There are also standard fire test procedures that can be used to determine the classification levels of aerosol products. Where such data exist, it should be used to identify that product's classification and serve as the basis for further modifications to the formulation-based criteria.

The most reliable test protocol currently available is the 12-pallet aerosol classification test, developed by Factory Mutual Research Corporation. This test consists of a 2-pallet × 2-pallet × 3-pallet high array, with sprinkler protection using upright sprinkler heads having 13 mm (0.64 in.) orifices (K-factor = 11.2), and 71°C (160°F) (RTI = 300) links, spaced 3 m × 3 m (10 ft × 10 ft) on a 7.6 m (25 ft) ceiling, with water pressure at a constant 345 kPa (50 psi) to provide 32.6 L/min · m^2 (0.8 gpm/ft^2).

Classification is determined from considering the "critical performance parameters" in the test, which include the number of sprinklers opened, maximum temperature of a steel beam on the ceiling, maximum plume velocity, maximum plume temperature, maximum heat flux, maximum weight loss rate, and net percent weight loss. The overall consideration in this test is whether control or suppression is achieved and the number of sprinklers that operated. Roughly speaking, fires involving Level 1 aerosol products are well controlled or suppressed; fires involving Level 2 aerosol products are well to marginally well controlled; and fires involving Level 3 aerosol products are not well controlled.

Annex D Flammability Labeling of Aerosol Products

This annex is not a part of the requirements of this NFPA document but is included for informational purposes only.

D.1 Precautionary labeling for aerosol products, including that for flammability hazards during use of the product, is regulated by several federal agencies, under a number of federal statutes. Labeling of aerosol pesticide products, including disinfectants and sanitizers as well as insecticides and herbicides, is strictly regulated by the U.S. Environmental Protection Agency (EPA) under the Federal Insecticide, Fungicide, and Rodenticide Act (FIFRA). Pesticide labeling regulations can be found in 40 CFR 162. Labeling of aerosol food, drug, and cosmetic products is regulated by the U.S. Food and Drug Administration (FDA), under The Federal Food, Drug, and Cosmetic Act (FFDCA). These regulations can be found in various parts of 21 CFR. The labeling of any consumer (household) aerosol products not already covered by the EPA or the FDA is regulated by the Consumer Product Safety Commission (CPSC), under the Federal Hazardous Substances Act (FHSA). These labeling regulations can be found in 16 CFR 1500.

The labeling of aerosol industrial and institutional products that do not fall under any of the above regulations is covered by the Occupational Safety and Health Administration (OSHA), under its hazard communications rules, in 29 CFR 1910.

Although there are many differences between the labeling requirements of the various agencies, there is some degree of consistency in their approach to evaluating and labeling aerosol products for their flammability hazard during use. They generally use the terms "flammable" or "extremely flammable" for aerosol products that meet certain flammability criteria and then mandate related precautionary language.

The principal test procedure for evaluating the in-use flammability of aerosol products is the flame extension test. In this test, the aerosol is sprayed through a flame and the length of the extension of the flame is measured. Any flashback of the flame toward the container valve is also noted. Some authorities also consider the flash point of the base product, although it is the position of the aerosol product industry that these data do not correlate closely with the in-use flammability of the total product.

It is important to understand that the in-use flammability of an aerosol product, as measured by the flame extension test, does not provide an adequate prediction of the fire hazard involved in the storage of the product. Thus, the product label cannot be used to determine whether the aerosol product should be handled as a Level 1, 2, or 3 product.

Annex E Loss Experience

This annex is not a part of the requirements of this NFPA document but is included for informational purposes only.

E.1 Fire and Explosion Incidents. Approximately one-third of the incidents involving aerosol products are fires that have occurred in warehouses. These facilities have included manufacturing warehouses, distribution warehouses, and public warehouses. The average loss was $1,220,000, but this does not include the two largest recorded losses, which together totaled $150,000,000. About 15 percent of the losses involved the disposal of aerosol products, either by incineration or by shredding and compacting. These incidents incurred an average loss of $150,000. Fires occur less frequently in this occupancy category. The largest explosion incident resulted in $1,000,000 in damage. Repair facilities account for another 15 percent of the losses, the average loss being $375,000. Eight percent of the losses occurred in aerosol-filling operations; these are evenly split between fires and explosions. Fire damage in these cases ranged from negligible to $250,000. Explosions in filling

Table E.1 Percentage Loss by Dollar Loss Category

Dollar Amount	Percent
$ 100,000	68
$ 250,000	52
$ 500,000	27
$1,000,000	27

operations also show a wide damage range, although the largest caused $11,000,000 in damage. See Table E.1.

Table E.1 shows that only 32 percent of the incidents had loss values less than $100,000 and that the median loss was $250,000.

E.2 Causes and Contributing Factors. Electrical equipment was cited as the ignition source in 15 percent of the incidents, except in propellant filling rooms, where electrical equipment was involved in almost every case. Smoking was cited in 8 percent of the incidents and arson in 5 percent. Almost half of the losses occurred in inadequately sprinklered or nonsprinklered properties.

E.3 Loss Incidents.

E.3.1 1979 Warehouse Fire. This nonfood supermarket warehouse was one story high, 244 m × 175 m (800 ft × 575 ft), and constructed of concrete block walls and a steel frame roof. Various commodities, including aerosol products, were stored up to 6 m (20 ft) high, in double-row racks. The building was protected by automatic sprinklers, using 100°C (212°F), 13 mm ($^{17}/_{32}$ in.) orifice heads. Sprinkler heads were spaced 9.3 m² (100 ft²) per head, designed for a density of 12.2 L/min·m² (0.3 gpm/ft²) over the most hydraulically remote 372 m² (4000 ft²). In-rack sprinklers were not provided.

An employee first noticed the fire behind a pallet on the first tier of a rack. He attempted extinguishment using a portable extinguisher, but was not successful. The fire spread to the next pallet load above, which held a Level 3 aerosol product, then rapidly up the face of the rack to the ceiling, creating dense black smoke that forced employees to abandon attempts to fight the fire. The roof of the warehouse began to fail as fire fighters arrived on the scene. The fire department was only able to connect to the pumper connection and use aerial snorkels. It took three days to finally extinguish the fire.

All the contents of the building were consumed. The roof and all of the walls collapsed. Property damage and business interruption were estimated at $30,000,000 and $20,000,000, respectively. Arson was suspected.

E.3.2 1982 Warehouse Fire. Levels 1, 2, and 3 aerosol products, as well as a variety of other products, were stored in this 111,480 m² (1.2 million ft²), 9 m (30 ft) high distribution center. Storage was 4.6 m (15 ft) high, in palletized arrays and in single- and double-row racks. The building was sprinklered, using 141°C (286°F), 13 mm ($^{17}/_{32}$ in.) orifice heads, designed for 16.3 L/min·m² (0.4 gpm/ft²) over 279 m² (3000 ft²). In-rack sprinklers were not provided.

An employee was checking paperwork while sitting in his fork-lift truck when he heard a carton fall from a pallet behind him. The carton contained a Level 3 aerosol product (carburetor cleaner). He heard a hissing sound, then saw flames almost immediately. By the time he was able to reach an extinguisher, flames had spread up the face of the stack from which the carton had fallen. Other employees responded, but heavy smoke forced them to evacuate.

The fire broke through the roof within 13 minutes. Responding fire fighters reported that aerosol containers were rupturing and rocketing, trailing burning contents. The fire burned out of control for 8½ hours. Final extinguishment was not achieved until 8 days later. The warehouse and its contents were totally destroyed.

In addition to the 40 to 50 pallets of carburetor cleaner located immediately adjacent to the ignition point, the warehouse contained an estimated 580,000 containers of Level 3 aerosol products and 480,000 containers of Level 2 aerosol products, as well as high flash point combustible liquids (motor oils), butane lighter refills, and small cylinders of propane for handheld torches.

Property damage exceeded $100,000,000.

Annex F Chemical Heat of Combustion

This annex is not a part of the requirements of this NFPA document but is included for informational purposes only.

F.1 Test data indicate that the overall fire hazard of an aerosol product is a function of the chemical heat of combustion. The chemical heat of combustion, H_c, in kilojoules per gram (kJ/g), is the product of the theoretical heat of combustion, H_{comb}, also in kilojoules per gram, and a combustion efficiency, usually less than 1.0. A typical combustion efficiency is 0.95, or 95 percent. For a product that consists of a number of components, the chemical heat of combustion is the summation of the weighted heats of combustion for the individual components as follows:

$$\Delta H_c (\text{product}) = \Sigma \left[I\% \times \Delta H_{c(I)} \right]$$

where:
ΔH_c = chemical heat of combustion (kJ/g)
$I\%$ = weight fraction of component I in product
$\Delta H_{c(I)}$ = chemical heat of combustion of component I (kJ/g)

Heats of combustion are available from standard chemical and chemical engineering references, such as *Perry's Chemical Engineers' Handbook,* and other standard references, such as the *Fire Protection Handbook* and *The SFPE Handbook of Fire Protection Engineering.*

Heats of combustion can also be determined by calculation or by appropriate test methods, such as ASTM D 240, *Standard Test Method for Heat of Combustion of Liquid Hydrocarbon Fuels by Bomb Calorimeter.*

Representative values are given in Table F.1(a). Where the chemical heat of combustion of a particular material is not readily available, or if the material is a minor component of the product mix, use the theoretical heat of combustion, ΔH_{comb}, or use 19,000 Btu/lb (43.7 kJ/g). This latter value is typical for hydrocarbons.

Table F.1(b) provides a cross-reference between Chemical Abstracts Service (CAS) numbers and the materials listed in Table F.1(a).

Examples of calculations of chemical heat of combustion are shown in F.1.1 through F.1.3.

Table F.1(a) Chemical Heat of Combustion for Representative Materials

Chemical Name	CAS Number[a]	Chemical Heat of Combustion[b] ΔH_c, kJ/g
Acetone	67-64-1	27.7
Acrylic Resin	—	c, d
Alkyd Resin	—	c, d
Aluminum	7429-90-5	c, d
Asphalt	8052-42-4	22.7
Barium Sulfate	7727-43-7	0.0
Benzidine (Yellow)	92-87-5	c, d
Butane	106-97-8	43.3
2-Butoxyethanol	111-76-2	29.6
Butyl Benzyl Phthalate	85-68-7	31.5
Calcium Carbonate	1317-65-3	0.0
Carbon Black	1333-86-4	c, d
Carbon Dioxide	124-38-9	0.0
1-Chloro-1,1-Difluoroethane (HCFC 142b)	75-68-3	3.3
Chromium Hydroxide	1308-14-1	0.0
Corn Oil	8001-30-7	35.3
Diacetone Alcohol	123-42-2	35.1
1,1-Dichloro-1-Fluoroethane	1717-00-6	2.9
Diethylene Glycol Methyl Ether	112-34-5	33.0
1,1-Difluoroethane (HFC 152a)	75-37-6	6.3
1,2-Dimethoxyethane	110-71-4	25.9
Dimethyl Ether	115-10-6	26.5
Dipropylene Glycol Methyl Ether	34590-94-8	32.2
Ethanol	64-17-15	24.7
Ethanol (95.6% Azeotrope)	64-17-15	23.6
2-Ethoxyethanol	110-80-5	25.9
2-Ethoxyethyl Acetate	111-15-9	30.9
Ethyl 3-Ethoxypropionate	763-69-9	32.0
Ethylbenzene	100-41-4	29.0
Ethylene Glycol	107-21-1	16.4
Ethylene Glycol Diacetate	111-55-7	32.0
Graphite	7782-42-5	c, d
Hexylene Glycol	107-41-5	28.5
Iron Oxide	1309-37-1	0.0
Isobutane, See 2-Methylpropane	—	
Isobutyl Alcohol	78-83-1	29.8
Isopropyl Acetate	108-21-4	25.5
Isopropyl Alcohol	67-63-0	27.4
Isopropyl Myristate	110-27-0	36.2
Isopropyl Palmitate	142-91-6	37.2
Kaolin Clay (Aluminum Silicate Hydroxide)	1332-58-7	0.0
Kerosene	8008-20-6	41.4
d-Limonene	5989-27-5	39.8
Liquids, Noncombustible/Nonflammable	—	0.0
Liquids, Noncontributory	—	c, d
Magnesium Silicate (Talc)	14807-96-6	0.0
Methanol	67-56-1	19.0
1-Methoxy-2-Propanol Acetate	108-65-6	30.9
Methyl Ethyl Ketone	78-93-3	30.6
Methyl Isopropyl Ketone	563-80-4	31.1
Methyl n-Amyl Ketone	110-43-0	35.0
Methylene Chloride	75-09-2	2.1
2-Methylpropane (Isobutane)	75-28-5	42.8
Mica (Mica Silicate)	12001-26-2	0.0
Mineral Oil	8012-95-1	31.5

Table F.1(a) *Continued*

Chemical Name	CAS Number[a]	Chemical Heat of Combustion[b] ΔH_c, kJ/g
Mineral Spirits (Petroleum Distillate)	64742-47-8	41.2
Mineral Spirits (Petroleum Distillate)	64742-88-7	41.2
N,N-Diethyl-m-Toluamide (Deet)	134-62-3	28.2
n-Butyl Acetate	123-86-4	27.6
n-Heptane	142-82-5	41.0
n-Hexane	110-54-3	41.1
n-Octyl Bicycloheptane Dicarboximide	113-48-4	30.0
Naphtha (High Flash)	8052-41-3	41.2
Naphtha (Petroleum Distillate)	8030-30-6	41.2
Naphtha, VM&P (Petroleum Distillate)	64742-95-6	41.2
Naphtha, VM&P (Petroleum Distillate)	64742-48-9	41.2
Naphtha, VM&P (Petroleum Distillate)	64742-94-5	41.2
Nitrogen	7727-37-9	0.0
Paraffin (Wax)	8002-74-2	c,d
Pentane	109-66-0	41.9
Perchloroethylene (Tetrachloroethylene)	127-18-4	c, d
Petroleum Distillate	64741-65-7	41.2
Phthalocyanine Blue	147-14-8	c, d
Phthalocyanine Green	1328-53-6	c, d
Piperonyl Butoxide	51-03-6	32.0
Polyoxyethlene Sorbitan Oleate	9005-65-6	c, d
Polyoxyethylene (20) Sorbitan Monolaurate	9005-64-5	c, d
Propane	74-98-6	44.0
Propylene Glycol	57-55-6	20.5
sec-Butyl Alcohol	78-92-2	39.9
Silica (Crystalline)	—	0.0
Silica, Amorphous Hydrated	7631-86-9	0.0
Silicone Oil	63148-58-3	c, d
Silicone Oil	63148-62-9	c, d
Solids, Noncombustible/Nonflammable	—	0.0
Solids, Noncontributory	—	c, d
Sorbitan Monolaurate	1338-39-2	37.9
Sorbitan Monopalmitate	26266-57-9	37.9
Styrene Butadiene Rubber	25038-32-8	c,d
Tin Oxide (Stannic Oxide)	18252-10-5	0.0
Titanium Dioxide	13463-67-7	0.0
Toluene	108-88-3	28.4
Triacetin	102-76-1	35.4
1,1,1-Trichloroethane	71-55-6	c, d
Trichloroethylene	79-01-6	c, d
1,2,4-Trimethylbenzene (Pseudocumene)	95-63-6	27.5
Water	7732-18-5	0.0
Xylene	1330-20-7	27.4
Zinc Oxide	1314-13-2	0.0

[a] Chemical Abstracts Service Registration Number.
[b] The theoretical heats of combustion and combustion efficiencies used to determine the chemical heats of combustion listed in this table are contained in the supporting documentation on file at NFPA.
[c] Materials that have either (1) a closed-cup flash point greater than 260°C (500°F), or (2) no fire point when tested in accordance with ASTM D 92, *Test Method for Flash and Fire Points by Cleveland Open Cup*, or (3) are combustible solids. Such materials contribute very little to the overall fire hazard of aerosol products in an actual fire, due to incomplete combustion or inconsistent burning behavior (i.e., the majority of the released material does not burn). Such materials are considered to be "noncontributory" to the overall determination of the product's level of classification. They can be ignored, or they can be assigned a chemical heat of combustion (ΔH_c) of 0 kJ/g.
Note: Footnote c will be in effect through 12/31/2011.

[d] Materials that either have no fire point when tested in accordance with ASTM D 92, *Test Method for Flash and Fire Points by Cleveland Open Cup*, or are combustible solids. Such materials contribute very little to the overall fire hazard of aerosol products in an actual fire, due to incomplete combustion or inconsistent burning behavior (i.e., the majority of the released material does not burn). Such materials are considered to be "noncontributory" to the overall determination of the product's level of classification. They can be ignored or they can be assigned a chemical heat of combustion (ΔH_c) of 0 kJ/g.
Note: Footnote d will be in effect as of 1/1/2012.

Table F.1(b) Cross-Reference Table — Chemical Abstracts Service (CAS) Numbers for Representative Materials in Table F.1(a)

CAS Number	Chemical Name
51-03-6	Piperonyl Butoxide
57-55-6	Propylene Glycol
64-17-15	Ethanol
64-17-15	Ethanol (95.6% Azeotrope)
67-56-1	Methanol
67-63-0	Isopropyl Alcohol
67-64-1	Acetone
71-55-6	1,1,1-Trichloroethane
74-98-6	Propane
75-09-2	Methylene Chloride
75-28-5	2-Methylpropane (Isobutane)
75-37-6	1,1-Difluoroethane (HFC 152a)
75-68-3	1-Chloro-1,1-Difluoroethane (HCFC 142b)
78-83-1	Isobutyl Alcohol
78-92-2	sec-Butyl Alcohol
78-93-3	Methyl Ethyl Ketone
79-01-6	Trichloroethylene
85-68-7	Butyl Benzyl Phthalate
92-87-5	Benzidine (Yellow)
95-63-6	1,2,4-Trimethylbenzene (Pseudocumene)
100-41-4	Ethylbenzene
102-76-1	Triacetin
106-97-8	Butane
107-21-1	Ethylene Glycol
107-41-5	Hexylene Glycol
108-21-4	Isopropyl Acetate
108-65-6	1-Methoxy-2-Propanol Acetate
108-88-3	Toluene
109-66-0	Pentane
110-27-0	Isopropyl Myristate
110-43-0	Methyl n-Amyl Ketone
110-54-3	n-Hexane
110-71-4	1,2-Dimethoxyethane
110-80-5	2-Ethoxyethanol
111-15-9	2-Ethoxyethyl Acetate
111-55-7	Ethylene Glycol Diacetate
111-76-2	2-Butoxyethanol
112-34-5	Diethylene Glycol Methyl Ether
113-48-4	n-Octyl Bicycloheptane Dicarboximide
115-10-6	Dimethyl Ether
123-42-2	Diacetone Alcohol
123-86-4	n-Butyl Acetate
124-38-9	Carbon Dioxide
127-18-4	Perchloroethylene (Tetrachloroethylene)
134-62-3	N,N-Diethyl-m-Toluamide (Deet)
142-82-5	n-Heptane
142-91-6	Isopropyl Palmitate
147-14-8	Phthalocyanine Blue

Table F.1(b) *Continued*

CAS Number	Chemical Name
563-80-4	Methyl Isopropyl Ketone
763-69-9	Ethyl 3-Ethoxypropionate
1308-14-1	Chromium Hydroxide
1309-37-1	Iron Oxide
1314-13-2	Zinc Oxide
1317-65-3	Calcium Carbonate
1328-53-6	Phthalocyanine Green
1330-20-7	Xylene
1332-58-7	Kaolin Clay (Aluminum Silicate Hydroxide)
1333-86-4	Carbon Black
1338-39-2	Sorbitan Monolaurate
1717-00-6	1,1-Dichloro-1-Fluoroethane
5989-27-5	d-Limonene
7429-90-5	Aluminum
7631-86-9	Silica, Amorphous Hydrated
7727-37-9	Nitrogen
7727-43-7	Barium Sulfate
7732-18-5	Water
7782-42-5	Graphite
8001-30-7	Corn Oil
8002-74-2	Paraffin (Wax)
8008-20-6	Kerosene
8012-95-1	Mineral Oil
8030-30-6	Naphtha (Petroleum Distillate)
8052-41-3	Naphtha (High Flash)
8052-42-4	Asphalt
9005-64-5	Polyoxyethylene (20) Sorbitan Monolaurate
9005-65-6	Polyoxyethlene Sorbitan Oleate
12001-26-2	Mica (Mica Silicate)
13463-67-7	Titanium Dioxide
14807-96-6	Magnesium Silicate (Talc)
18252-10-5	Tin Oxide (Stannic Oxide)
25038-32-8	Styrene Butadiene Rubber
26266-57-9	Sorbitan Monopalmitate
34590-94-8	Dipropylene Glycol Methyl Ether
63148-58-3	Silicone Oil
63148-62-9	Silicone Oil
64741-65-7	Petroleum Distillate
64742-47-8	Mineral Spirits (Petroleum Distillate)
64742-48-9	Naphtha, VM&P (Petroleum Distillate)
64742-88-7	Mineral Spirits (Petroleum Distillate)
64742-94-5	Naphtha, VM&P (Petroleum Distillate)
64742-95-6	Naphtha, VM&P (Petroleum Distillate)

F.1.1 Example 1. See Table F.1.1.

F.1.2 Example 2. See Table F.1.2.

F.1.3 Example 3. See Table F.1.3.

Table F.1.1 Typical Level 1 Aerosol Product

Ingredient	Weight (%)	ΔH_c of Ingredient (kJ)	Weight % × ΔH_c (kJ)
Isobutane	30	42.7	12.8
Water	69		0
Fragrance, etc.	1	43.7*	0.4
			Total = 13.2 kJ

For U.S. customary units, 1 kJ = 0.95 Btu.

*Since the fragrance constitutes a small proportion of the total, 43.7 kJ/g was used instead of actually determining or calculating the heat of combustion. In this example, the resulting classification of the aerosol product was not affected. However, with other products, this might not be the case and actual calculation of or testing for the heat of combustion might have to be done.

Table F.1.2 Typical Level 2 Aerosol Product

Ingredient	Weight (%)	ΔH_c of Ingredient (kJ)	Weight % × ΔH_c (kJ)
Isobutane	20	42.7	8.5
Ethanol	60	25.5	15.3
Water		19	0
Fragrance, Surfactant, Corrosion Inhibitors, or other minor ingredients	1	43.7*	0.4
			Total = 24.2 kJ

For U.S. customary units, 1 kJ = 0.95 Btu.

*Since these minor ingredients constitute a small proportion of the total, 43.7 kJ/g was used instead of actually determining or calculating the heat of combustion. In this example, the resulting classification of the aerosol product was not affected. However, with other products, this might not be the case and actual calculation of or testing for the heat of combustion might have to be done.

Table F.1.3 Typical Level 3 Aerosol Product

Ingredient	Weight (%)	ΔH_c of Ingredient (kJ)	Weight % × ΔH_c (kJ)
Isobutane	25	42.7	10.7
Propane	10	43.7	4.4
Toluene	25	27.8	7.0
Acetone	15	27.9	4.2
Methyl Ethyl Ketone	15	30.7	4.6
Pigments (Titanium Dioxide), etc.	10	0	0
			Total = 30.9 kJ

For U.S. customary units, 1 kJ = 0.95 Btu.

Annex G Sample Ordinance Adopting NFPA 30B

This annex is not a part of the requirements of this NFPA document but is included for informational purposes only.

G.1 The following sample ordinance is provided to assist a jurisdiction in the adoption of this code and is not part of this code.

ORDINANCE NO. _____

An ordinance of the *[jurisdiction]* adopting the *[year]* edition of NFPA *[document number]*, *[complete document title]* documents listed in Chapter 2 of that *[code, standard]*; prescribing regulations governing conditions hazardous to life and property from fire or explosion; providing for the issuance of permits and collection of fees; repealing Ordinance No. _____ of the *[jurisdiction]* and all other ordinances and parts of ordinances in conflict therewith; providing a penalty; providing a severability clause; and providing for publication; and providing an effective date.

BE IT ORDAINED BY THE *[governing body]* OF THE *[jurisdiction]*:

SECTION 1 That the *[complete document title]* and documents adopted by Chapter 2, three (3) copies of which are on file and are open to inspection by the public in the office of the *[jurisdiction's keeper of records]* of the *[jurisdiction]*, are hereby adopted and incorporated into this ordinance as fully as if set out at length herein, and from the date on which this ordinance shall take effect, the provisions thereof shall be controlling within the limits of the *[jurisdiction]*. The same are hereby adopted as the *[code, standard]* of the *[jurisdiction]* for the purpose of prescribing regulations governing conditions hazardous to life and property from fire or explosion and providing for issuance of permits and collection of fees.

SECTION 2 Any person who shall violate any provision of this code or standard hereby adopted or fail to comply therewith; or who shall violate or fail to comply with any order made thereunder; or who shall build in violation of any detailed statement of specifications or plans submitted and approved thereunder; or failed to operate in accordance with any certificate or permit issued thereunder; and from which no appeal has been taken; or who shall fail to comply with such an order as affirmed or modified by or by a court of competent jurisdiction, within the time fixed herein, shall severally for each and every such violation and noncompliance, respectively, be guilty of a misdemeanor, punishable by a fine of not less than $_____ nor more than $_____ or by imprisonment for not less than _____ days nor more than _____ days or by both such fine and imprisonment. The imposition of one penalty for any violation shall not excuse the violation or permit it to continue; and all such persons shall be required to correct or remedy such violations or defects within a reasonable time; and when not otherwise specified the application of the above penalty shall not be held to prevent the enforced removal of prohibited conditions. Each day that prohibited conditions are maintained shall constitute a separate offense.

SECTION 3 Additions, insertions, and changes — that the *[year]* edition of NFPA *[document number]*, *[complete document title]* is amended and changed in the following respects:

List Amendments

SECTION 4 That ordinance No. _____ of *[jurisdiction]* entitled *[fill in the title of the ordinance or ordinances in effect at the present time]* and all other ordinances or parts of ordinances in conflict herewith are hereby repealed.

SECTION 5 That if any section, subsection, sentence, clause, or phrase of this ordinance is, for any reason, held to be invalid or unconstitutional, such decision shall not affect the validity or constitutionality of the remaining portions of this ordinance. The *[governing body]* hereby declares that it would have passed this ordinance, and each section, subsection, clause, or phrase hereof, irrespective of the fact that any one or more sections, subsections, sentences, clauses, and phrases be declared unconstitutional.

SECTION 6 That the *[jurisdiction's keeper of records]* is hereby ordered and directed to cause this ordinance to be published.

[NOTE: An additional provision may be required to direct the number of times the ordinance is to be published and to specify that it is to be in a newspaper in general circulation. Posting may also be required.]

SECTION 7 That this ordinance and the rules, regulations, provisions, requirements, orders, and matters established and adopted hereby shall take effect and be in full force and effect *[time period]* from and after the date of its final passage and adoption.

Annex H Informational References

H.1 Referenced Publications. The documents or portions thereof listed in this annex are referenced within the informational sections of this code and are not part of the requirements of this document unless also listed in Chapter 2 for other reasons.

H.1.1 NFPA Publications. National Fire Protection Association, 1 Batterymarch Park, Quincy, MA 02169-7471.

NFPA 10, *Standard for Portable Fire Extinguishers*, 2010 edition.

NFPA 13, *Standard for the Installation of Sprinkler Systems*, 2010 edition.

NFPA 15, *Standard for Water Spray Fixed Systems for Fire Protection*, 2007 edition.

NFPA 30, *Flammable and Combustible Liquids Code*, 2008 edition.

NFPA 51B, *Standard for Fire Prevention During Welding, Cutting, and Other Hot Work*, 2009 edition.

NFPA 58, *Liquefied Petroleum Gas Code*, 2011 edition.

NFPA 68, *Standard on Explosion Protection by Deflagration Venting*, 2007 edition.

NFPA 69, *Standard on Explosion Prevention Systems*, 2008 edition.

NFPA 77, *Recommended Practice on Static Electricity*, 2007 edition.

NFPA 80A, *Recommended Practice for Protection of Buildings from Exterior Fire Exposures*, 2007 edition.

NFPA 91, *Standard for Exhaust Systems for Air Conveying of Vapors, Gases, Mists, and Noncombustible Particulate Solids*, 2010 edition.

NFPA 497, *Recommended Practice for the Classification of Flammable Liquids, Gases, or Vapors and of Hazardous (Classified) Locations for Electrical Installations in Chemical Process Areas*, 2008 edition.

Fire Protection Handbook, 19th edition, 2003.

DiNenno, P. J., et al, *The SFPE Handbook of Fire Protection Engineering*, 2nd edition, National Fire Protection Association, Quincy, MA, 1995.

H.1.2 Other Publications.

H.1.2.1 ASTM Publications. ASTM International, 100 Barr Harbor Drive, P.O. Box C700, West Conshohocken, PA 19428-2959.

ASTM D 92, *Test Method for Flash and Fire Points by Cleveland Open Cup*, 2005.

ASTM D 240, *Standard Test Method for Heat of Combustion of Liquid Hydrocarbon Fuels by Bomb Calorimeter*, 2007.

ASTM D 3064, *Standard Definitions of Terms and Nomenclature Relating to Aerosol Products*, 2008.

H.1.2.2 CBPA Publications. Consumer Specialty Products Association Inc., 1913 I Street N.W., Washington, DC 20006.

"An Industry Responds: A Technical History of the CSMA Aerosol Warehouse Storage Fire Protection Research Program."

H.1.2.3 FMGR Publications. FM Global Research, FM Global, 1301 Atwood Avenue, P.O. Box 7500, Johnston, RI 02919.

"Full-Scale Fire Tests: Sprinkler Protection for Rack Storage of Plastic-Wrapped (Uncartoned) Aerosols," 2005.

H.1.2.4 UL Publications. Underwriters Laboratories Inc., 333 Pfingsten Road, Northbrook, IL 60062-2096.

"Large Drop Sprinkler Protection of Palletized Storage of Aerosols in Plastic Containers on Wood Pallets Testing Result," 2009.

"Palletized Plastic Aerosol Storage Testing Result," 2008.

H.1.2.5 U.S. Government Publications. U.S. Government Printing Office, Washington, DC 20402.

Title 16, Code of Federal Regulations, Commercial Practices, Part 1500.

Title 21, Code of Federal Regulations, Food and Drugs.

Title 29, Code of Federal Regulations, Labor, Part 1910.

Title 40, Code of Federal Regulations, Protection of Environment, Part 162.

Title 49, Code of Federal Regulations, Transportation.

H.1.2.6 Other Publications. Perry, R. H., and D. W. Green, *Perry's Chemical Engineers' Handbook*, 6th edition, McGraw Hill, New York, NY, 1984.

H.2 Informational References. (Reserved)

H.3 References for Extracts in Informational Sections. NFPA 30, *Flammable and Combustible Liquids Code*, 2008 edition.

Index

Copyright © 2010 National Fire Protection Association. All Rights Reserved.

The copyright in this index is separate and distinct from the copyright in the document that it indexes. The licensing provisions set forth for the document are not applicable to this index. This index may not be reproduced in whole or in part by any means without the express written permission of NFPA.

-A-

Administration .... Chap. 1
   Application 1.3
   Classification of Aerosol Products in Metal Containers
      and Plastic or Glass Containers Less Than or
      Equal to 118 ml (4 fl oz) 1.7, A.1.7
      Level 1 Aerosol Products 1.7.2
      Level 2 Aerosol Products 1.7.3
      Level 3 Aerosol Products 1.7.4
   Enforcement 1.6
   Equivalency 1.5
   Marking of Packages of Aerosol Products 1.8
   Purpose 1.2, A.1.2
   Retroactivity 1.4, A.1.4
   Scope 1.1
Aerosol
   Definition 3.3.1, A.3.3.1
Aerosol Container
   Definition 3.3.2, A.3.3.2
Aerosol Propellant
   Definition 3.3.3, A.3.3.3
Approved
   Definition 3.2.1, A.3.2.1
Authority Having Jurisdiction (AHJ)
   Definition 3.2.2, A.3.2.2

-B-

Back Stock Area
   Definition 3.3.4
Base Product (Concentrate)
   Definition 3.3.5, A.3.3.5
Base Product Filler (Concentrate Filler)
   Definition 3.4.1
Basement
   Definition 3.3.6
Basic Requirements .... Chap. 4
   Building Construction 4.2
      Means of Egress 4.2.2
   Electrical Installations 4.3
   Fire Alarms 4.7
   Fire Protection 4.6
      Automatic Sprinkler Protection 4.6.1
      Portable Fire Extinguishers 4.6.3
      Standpipe and Hose System 4.6.2
      Water Supplies 4.6.4
   Flammable Liquids and Gases 4.5
   Heating Equipment 4.4
   Site Requirements 4.1
   Sources of Ignition 4.8
Bonding
   Definition 3.3.7
Button Tipper (Actuator Placer)
   Definition 3.4.2, A.3.4.2

-C-

Carton
   Definition 3.3.8
Chemical Heat of Combustion .... Annex F
Code
   Definition 3.2.3, A.3.2.3
Cold Filling
   Definition 3.3.9, A.3.3.9
Combustion Efficiency
   Definition 3.3.10

-D-

Damage-Limiting Construction
   Definition 3.3.11
Definitions .... Chap. 3
Determining the Classification Level of Aerosol Products
      in Metal Containers .... Annex C

-E-

Encapsulation
   Definition 3.3.12
Explanatory Material .... Annex A

-F-

Fire Area
   Definition 3.3.13
Flammability Labeling of Aerosol Products .... Annex D
Flammable Propellant
   Definition 3.3.14
Fume Incinerator
   Definition 3.4.3

-G-

Grounding
   Definition 3.3.15

-H-

Heat of Combustion
   Chemical Heat of Combustion (Hc)
      Definition 3.3.16.1
   Definition 3.3.16
   Theoretical Heat of Combustion
      Definition 3.3.16.2
Horizontal Barrier
   Definition 3.3.17

-I-

Informational References .... Annex H
Inside Liquid Storage Area
   Definition 3.3.18

-L-

(Liquid Storage) Control Area
   Definition 3.3.19
Liquid Storage Room
   Definition 3.3.20
Liquid Warehouse
   Definition 3.3.21
Liquids
   Combustible Liquid
      Definition 3.3.22.1, A.3.3.22.1
   Definition 3.3.22
   Flammable Liquid
      Definition 3.3.22.2, A.3.3.22.2
   Unstable Liquid
      Definition 3.3.22.3
Local Ventilation
   Definition 3.4.4
Loss Experience .... Annex E

-M-

Manufacturing Facilities .... Chap. 5
   Aerosol Product Laboratories 5.15
   Automatic Sprinkler Protection 5.8
   Basic Requirements 5.2
      Separation of Flammable Propellant Charging
         and Pump Rooms 5.2.4
   Building Construction 5.3, A.5.3
      Damage-Limiting Construction 5.3.4
   Combustible Gas Detection Systems 5.7, A.5.7
   Control of Static Electricity 5.6, A.5.6
   Deflagration Suppression Systems 5.11
   Electrical Equipment 5.5
   Equipment Interlocks 5.12
   Fixed Extinguishing Systems 5.9
   Process Operating Requirements 5.13
      Crimper Vacuum Pump Discharge Vent 5.13.2
      Flammable Liquid Propellant Pump 5.13.4
      Packaging and Conveyor System 5.13.1
      Propellant Charging Equipment 5.13.3
      Test Baths 5.13.5
   Scope 5.1, A.5.1
   Shrink-Wrapping of Aerosol Products 5.14, A.5.14
   Spill Control 5.10
   Ventilation 5.4
Mechanism of Fire Growth in Aerosol Containers .... Annex B
Mercantile Occupancies .... Chap. 7
   Back Stock Storage Areas 7.3
   Sales Display Areas — Aerosol Storage Exceeding
      2.4 m (8 ft) High 7.2
      Protection 7.2.3
   Sales Display Areas — Aerosol Storage Not Exceeding
      2.4 m (8 ft) High 7.1
   Special Protection Design 7.4
Mercantile Occupancy
   Definition 3.3.23

-N-

Net Weight
   Definition 3.3.24, A.3.3.24
Noncommunicating Wall
   Definition 3.3.25

-O-

Operations and Maintenance .... Chap. 8
   Aisles 8.4
   Control of Ignition Sources 8.3
      Sources of Ignition 8.3.1
   Inspection and Maintenance 8.6
      Maintenance 8.6.3
   Means of Egress 8.1
   Powered Industrial Trucks 8.2
      Loads 8.2.4
   Static Electricity 8.7, A.8.7
   Waste Disposal 8.5

-P-

Packaging Types
   Definition 3.3.26
   Packaging Type — Display Cut
      Definition 3.3.26.2
   Packaging Type — Cartoned
      Definition 3.3.26.1
   Packaging Type — Uncartoned
      Definition 3.3.26.3
Propellant Charging Pump (Charging Pump)
   Definition 3.4.5
Propellant Charging Room (Gas House, Gassing Room)
   Definition 3.4.6, A.3.4.6

Propellant Filler (Gasser, Propellant Charger)
   Definition 3.4.7, A.3.4.7
Protection for Exposures
   Definition 3.3.27
Pump Room
   Definition 3.4.8

-R-

Rack
   Definition 3.3.28, A.3.3.28
   Open Rack
      Definition 3.3.28.1
   Rack Shelf Area
      Definition 3.3.28.2
   Slatted Shelf Rack
      Definition 3.3.28.3
   Solid Shelf Rack
      Definition 3.3.28.4
Radiant Energy-Sensing Fire Detector
   Definition 3.4.9
Referenced Publications .... Chap. 2
   General 2.1
   NFPA Publications 2.2
   Other Publications 2.3
   References for Extracts in Mandatory Sections 2.4
Reject Container Receptacle
   Definition 3.4.10

-S-

Sales Display Area
   Definition 3.3.29
Sample Ordinance Adopting NFPA 30B .... Annex G
Separate Inside Storage Area
   Definition 3.3.30
   Separate Inside Storage Area — Inside Room
      Definition 3.3.30.4
   Separate Inside Storage Area — Cut-Off Room
      Definition 3.3.30.2
   Separate Inside Storage Area — Attached Building
      Definition 3.3.30.1
   Separate Inside Storage Area — Fenced Enclosure
      Definition 3.3.30.3
Shall
   Definition 3.2.4
Should
   Definition 3.2.5
Sprinklers
   Definition 3.3.31
   Early Suppression Fast-Response (ESFR) Sprinklers
      Definition 3.3.31.1
   Face Sprinklers
      Definition 3.3.31.2, A.3.3.31.2
Storage in Warehouses and Storage Areas .... Chap. 6
   Basic Requirements 6.1
   Storage of Level 1 Aerosol Products 6.2, A.6.2
   Storage of Level 2 and Level 3 Aerosol Products 6.3
      Aerosol Warehouses 6.3.6
      Fire Protection — Basic Requirements 6.3.2
      Limited-Quantity Storage in General-Purpose
         Warehouses 6.3.4
      Limited-Quantity Storage in Occupancies Other Than
         Warehouses 6.3.3
      Outdoor Storage 6.3.9
      Segregated Aerosol Product Storage Areas in General-Purpose
         Warehouses 6.3.5
      Storage of Aerosol Products in Inside Liquid Storage
         Areas, Liquid Storage Rooms, and Liquid Storage
         Control Areas 6.3.7
      Storage of Aerosol Products in Liquid Warehouses 6.3.8

-T-

Test Bath (Hot Tank, Water Bath)
　Definition 3.4.11, A.3.4.11

-V-

Vacuum Pump
　Definition 3.4.12
Valve Crimper (Crimper)
　Definition 3.4.13

-W-

Warehouse
　Aerosol Warehouse
　　Definition 3.3.32.1
　Definition 3.3.32
　General-Purpose Warehouse
　　Definition 3.3.32.2
　Liquid Warehouse
　　Definition 3.3.32.3

Sequence of Events Leading to Issuance of an NFPA Committee Document

Step 1: Call for Proposals

- Proposed new Document or new edition of an existing Document is entered into one of two yearly revision cycles, and a Call for Proposals is published.

Step 2: Report on Proposals (ROP)

- Committee meets to act on Proposals, to develop its own Proposals, and to prepare its Report.
- Committee votes by written ballot on Proposals. If two-thirds approve, Report goes forward. Lacking two-thirds approval, Report returns to Committee.
- Report on Proposals (ROP) is published for public review and comment.

Step 3: Report on Comments (ROC)

- Committee meets to act on Public Comments to develop its own Comments, and to prepare its report.
- Committee votes by written ballot on Comments. If two-thirds approve, Report goes forward. Lacking two-thirds approval, Report returns to Committee.
- Report on Comments (ROC) is published for public review.

Step 4: Technical Report Session

- "*Notices of intent to make a motion*" are filed, are reviewed, and valid motions are certified for presentation at the Technical Report Session. ("Consent Documents" that have no certified motions bypass the Technical Report Session and proceed to the Standards Council for issuance.)
- NFPA membership meets each June at the Annual Meeting Technical Report Session and acts on Technical Committee Reports (ROP and ROC) for Documents with "certified amending motions."
- Committee(s) vote on any amendments to Report approved at NFPA Annual Membership Meeting.

Step 5: Standards Council Issuance

- Notification of intent to file an appeal to the Standards Council on Association action must be filed within 20 days of the NFPA Annual Membership Meeting.
- Standards Council decides, based on all evidence, whether or not to issue Document or to take other action, including hearing any appeals.

Committee Membership Classifications

The following classifications apply to Technical Committee members and represent their principal interest in the activity of the committee.

M   *Manufacturer:* A representative of a maker or marketer of a product, assembly, or system, or portion thereof, that is affected by the standard.

U   *User:* A representative of an entity that is subject to the provisions of the standard or that voluntarily uses the standard.

I/M   *Installer/Maintainer:* A representative of an entity that is in the business of installing or maintaining a product, assembly, or system affected by the standard.

L   *Labor:* A labor representative or employee concerned with safety in the workplace.

R/T   *Applied Research/Testing Laboratory:* A representative of an independent testing laboratory or independent applied research organization that promulgates and/or enforces standards.

E   *Enforcing Authority:* A representative of an agency or an organization that promulgates and/or enforces standards.

I   *Insurance:* A representative of an insurance company, broker, agent, bureau, or inspection agency.

C   *Consumer:* A person who is, or represents, the ultimate purchaser of a product, system, or service affected by the standard, but who is not included in the *User* classification.

SE   *Special Expert:* A person not representing any of the previous classifications, but who has a special expertise in the scope of the standard or portion thereof.

NOTES;
1. "Standard" connotes code, standard, recommended practice, or guide.
2. A representative includes an employee.
3. While these classifications will be used by the Standards Council to achieve a balance for Technical Committees, the Standards Council may determine that new classifications of members or unique interests need representation in order to foster the best possible committee deliberations on any project. In this connection, the Standards Council may make appointments as it deems appropriate in the public interest, such as the classification of "Utilities" in the National Electrical Code Committee.
4. Representatives of subsidiaries of any group are generally considered to have the same classification as the parent organization.

NFPA Document Proposal Form

NOTE: All Proposals must be received by 5:00 pm EST/EDST on the published Proposal Closing Date.

For further information on the standards-making process, please contact the Codes and Standards Administration at 617-984-7249 or visit www.nfpa.org/codes.

For technical assistance, please call NFPA at 1-800-344-3555.

FOR OFFICE USE ONLY
Log #: _____
Date Rec'd: _____

Please indicate in which format you wish to receive your ROP/ROC ☐ electronic ☐ paper ☒ download
(Note: If choosing the download option, you must view the ROP/ROC from our website; no copy will be sent to you.)

Date April 1, 200X **Name** John J. Doe **Tel. No.** 716-555-1234
Company Air Canada Pilot's Association **Email**
Street Address 123 Summer Street Lane **City** Lewiston **State** NY **Zip** 14092

***If you wish to receive a hard copy, a street address MUST be provided. Deliveries cannot be made to PO boxes.**

Please indicate organization represented (if any) _____

1. (a) NFPA Document Title National Fuel Gas Code   NFPA No. & Year 54, 200X Edition
   (b) Section/Paragraph 3.3

2. **Proposal Recommends** (check one): ☐ new text ☒ revised text ☐ deleted text

3. **Proposal** (include proposed new or revised wording, or identification of wording to be deleted): [Note: Proposed text should be in legislative format; i.e., use underscore to denote wording to be inserted (inserted wording) and strike-through to denote wording to be deleted (deleted wording).]

Revise definition of effective ground-fault current path to read:

3.3.78 Effective Ground-Fault Current Path. An intentionally constructed, permanent, low impedance electrically conductive path designed and intended to carry underground electric fault current conditions from the point of a ground fault on a wiring system to the electrical supply source.

4. **Statement of Problem and Substantiation for Proposal:** (Note: State the problem that would be resolved by your recommendation; give the specific reason for your Proposal, including copies of tests, research papers, fire experience, etc. If more than 200 words, it may be abstracted for publication.)

Change uses proper electrical terms.

5. **Copyright Assignment**

   (a) ☐ I am the author of the text or other material (such as illustrations, graphs) proposed in the Proposal.

   (b) ☒ Some or all of the text or other material proposed in this Proposal was not authored by me. Its source is as follows: (please identify which material and provide complete information on its source)

   ABC Co.

I hereby grant and assign to the NFPA all and full rights in copyright in this Proposal and understand that I acquire no rights in any publication of NFPA in which this Proposal in this or another similar or analogous form is used. Except to the extent that I do not have authority to make an assignment in materials that I have identified in (b) above, I hereby warrant that I am the author of this Proposal and that I have full power and authority to enter into this assignment.

Signature (Required) _____

PLEASE USE SEPARATE FORM FOR EACH PROPOSAL

Mail to: Secretary, Standards Council · National Fire Protection Association
1 Batterymarch Park · Quincy, MA 02169-7471 OR
Fax to: (617) 770-3500 OR Email to: proposals_comments@nfpa.org

6/09-B

NFPA Document Proposal Form

NOTE: All Proposals must be received by 5:00 pm EST/EDST on the published Proposal Closing Date.

For further information on the standards-making process, please contact the Codes and Standards Administration at 617-984-7249 or visit www.nfpa.org/codes.

For technical assistance, please call NFPA at 1-800-344-3555.

FOR OFFICE USE ONLY
Log #: _____
Date Rec'd: _____

Please indicate in which format you wish to receive your ROP/ROC ☐ electronic ☐ paper ☐ download
(Note: If choosing the download option, you must view the ROP/ROC from our website; no copy will be sent to you.)

Date _____ Name _____ Tel. No. _____
Company _____ Email _____
Street Address _____ City _____ State _____ Zip _____

***If you wish to receive a hard copy, a street address MUST be provided. Deliveries cannot be made to PO boxes.

Please indicate organization represented (if any) _____

1. (a) NFPA Document Title _____ NFPA No. & Year _____
   (b) Section/Paragraph _____

2. Proposal Recommends (check one): ☐ new text   ☐ revised text   ☐ deleted text

3. Proposal (include proposed new or revised wording, or identification of wording to be deleted): [Note: Proposed text should be in legislative format; i.e., use underscore to denote wording to be inserted (inserted wording) and strike-through to denote wording to be deleted (deleted wording).]

4. Statement of Problem and Substantiation for Proposal: (Note: State the problem that would be resolved by your recommendation; give the specific reason for your Proposal, including copies of tests, research papers, fire experience, etc. If more than 200 words, it may be abstracted for publication.)

5. Copyright Assignment

   (a) ☐ I am the author of the text or other material (such as illustrations, graphs) proposed in the Proposal.

   (b) ☐ Some or all of the text or other material proposed in this Proposal was not authored by me. Its source is as follows: (please identify which material and provide complete information on its source)

I hereby grant and assign to the NFPA all and full rights in copyright in this Proposal and understand that I acquire no rights in any publication of NFPA in which this Proposal in this or another similar or analogous form is used. Except to the extent that I do not have authority to make an assignment in materials that I have identified in (b) above, I hereby warrant that I am the author of this Proposal and that I have full power and authority to enter into this assignment.

Signature (Required) _____

PLEASE USE SEPARATE FORM FOR EACH PROPOSAL

Mail to: Secretary, Standards Council · National Fire Protection Association
1 Batterymarch Park · Quincy, MA 02169-7471 OR
Fax to: (617) 770-3500 OR Email to: proposals_comments@nfpa.org

6/09-C